The Flying Dictionary

THE FLYING DICTIONARY
A Captivating and Unparalleled Primer
(Air Crashes and Miracle Landings)
[See below]

by
Christopher Bartlett

Originally created for

AIR CRASHES AND MIRACLE LANDINGS:
SIXTY NARRATIVES
(How, When ... and Most Importantly Why)

ISBN 978-0-9560723-2-0
Trade paperback 6" x 9" 370 pages
on high quality white paper

Published by
OpenHatch Books
www.openhatchbooks.com

Printed in the U.S. and U.K. on high quality white paper

ISBN 978-0-9560723-3-7

Published by
OpenHatch Books,
12 SL9 8NR, Buckinghamshire, U.K.
www.openhatchbooks.com

(August 2010)

Dedicated to
John Hawkins

The Author

Christopher Bartlett initially trained as a mining engineer, a field where ensuring compliance with safety standards is of prime importance. His passion, however, has been flying, and notably air safety.

This was engendered as an Air Cadet during his youth and as an early member of the British Interplanetary Society, as well as in the course of sessions on fighter simulators at the Air Ministry. He completed his two years' military service in the British Royal Air Force.

After taking a degree in Modern Chinese and Japanese at the School of Oriental and African Studies, London University, he became, amongst other things, a professional translator of Japanese scientific and technical material. This included Japanese rocket tests. He also wrote for magazines in the Far East.

His fluency and understanding of English, French, and Japanese enabled him to undertake research based on material published in its original format and note opinions and facts that have previously not been widely publicized.

Preface

Every effort has been taken to make the technical entries as balanced and as objective as possible.

However, to avoid the book becoming long and tedious, the entries for manufacturers and particular aircraft are largely limited to observations adding essential and sometimes provocative perspective.

In addition, some well-known aircraft—notably Russian—have been omitted as they did not feature in *Air Crashes and Miracle Landings* and are not so often used by likely readers.

Anyone noting the absence of key terms—or feeling that an entry grossly misrepresents an organization or individual—is welcome to email his or her observations to comments@openhatchbooks.com. These will be taken into account when updating or publishing future editions.

Christopher Bartlett

Acknowledgements

The acknowledgments in *Air Crashes and Miracle Landings* apply equally to this volume.

DICTIONARY

> Unusual mid-sentence capitalization of terms usually indicates they have their own individual entry.
>
> Unless otherwise specified, the year in square brackets following an aircraft type indicates when it entered service, and not the date of the first flight. The subsequent number is the number (including variants) produced, with a plus (+) sign usually indicating production is ongoing.

.303 (bullet)

In 1891 or 1892, the British Army finally replaced the traditional black powder used in the original .303 inch round with a much more effective smokeless Cordite propellant. The advantages included a flatter trajectory and greater accuracy. Yet, while the metal-clad bullet stood a greater likelihood of hitting its target, the wound it left on traversing soft tissue was usually relatively minor, so much so that several hits often failed to prove fatal or incapacitating.

In an attempt to rectify this, the Dum-Dum arsenal in India removed the tip of the metal-jacketed bullet to expose the soft lead core, which they then partially hollowed out. This *expanding-on-impact* round proved exceedingly effective, and while its use was limited to the Indian theater (which included Afghanistan), less destructive hollow-tipped versions of the .303 were developed for use elsewhere.

Dum-Dum bullets soon became controversial, particularly in view of the prospect of their use against Europeans, let alone against the Boers in South Africa. As a result, the British felt obliged to sign up to the Hague Convention in 1899 banning their use.

However, the British and others largely circumvented the Convention by developing an 'improved' .303 round, called the Mark VII, with the front third made of extremely light material such as aluminum or wood. Besides reducing total weight to give increased muzzle velocity and accuracy, this made the projectile tail-heavy, so that it would topple on slowing in human tissue, thus increasing the severity of the wound.

The round that ultimately killed the German World War I Fighter Ace, the Red Baron, would have been this Mark VII version, used in both rifles and machine guns on the Allied side. See Hydrostatic Shock.

1969

By an almost unbelievable coincidence, 1969 was the year that

- Neil Armstrong took man's first steps on the Moon. twelve years after Sputnik 1, the first Russian satellite, had been launched.
- The Boeing 747 made its maiden flight
- The Anglo-French supersonic Concorde airliner also made its maiden flight

367-80 (Boeing Dash-80) [First flight 1954]

Prototype four-engine jet aircraft that first flew on July 15, 1954, and was the forerunner to the KC-135 Stratotanker and the Boeing 707.

7x7

Boeing jet airliners begin with a "7" simply because that was the number the company used to designate a jet as opposed to say a piston-engine aircraft. Apparently, 707 rather than 700 or 701 was chosen for the 707, to avoid the appearance that it was the first one and because it sounded better. Boeing's airliners are so well known that the 7x7 formula has since become almost proprietary with people omitting the Boeing prefix when referring to them.

While Boeing is also well-known for its military aircraft such as the B-52 and B-17, the "B" does not stand for Boeing. See Designations (US military aircraft).

707 (Boeing 707) [1958] 1,000+

and KC-135 Stratotanker [1957] 800+

The Boeing 707 that transformed long-haul air travel was a said to have been a brave *betting-the-company* venture.

Yet the bet was not as wild as it appeared, as it was based on investment and design work on the above-mentioned 367-80 (Dash-80) prototype for a jet-engine mid-air refueling platform. There was a crying need for this as the newly developed jet engine bombers had to lose height and slow almost to stalling speed to be refueled by traditional piston engine tankers.

Having developed the refueling boom used by those piston engine tankers, Boeing duly received orders for the KC-135 Stratotanker, which was to prove a greater money-spinner, since the arrival on the commercial scene of competitors, such as Douglas with the DC-8, with a wider cabin and greater payload, necessitated a number of expensive modifications to the airliner variant.

The 707 entered commercial service in 1958 with Pan Am across the North Atlantic, just a few weeks after the much smaller and more expensive to run Comet 3 had tried to rejoin the race it had led prior to the disasters to the Comet 1. See Comet.

Douglas, a longtime favorite of the U.S. civil aviation industry, had held back on developing a jet engine airliner in the expectation that economical turboprops would be the next step. However, once a reliable and much faster jetliner arrived on the scene, they were obliged to follow suit. As in the case of the Boeing 747, Pan Am's Juan Trippe was the prime mover as launch customer for the 707 (and for the Douglas' DC-8). Pan Am's exclusive jet flights had the then unheard of load factors of 90%.

727 (Boeing 727) [1967] 1,381

When introduced into commercial service in December 1967, the Boeing 727 was the first trijet, and no one imagined it would become one of the most successful aircraft ever. Production ceased in August 1984. As a short to medium range airliner, it was widely used on U.S. domestic routes via secondary airports for which it was tailored. Overseas airlines also had many similar routes where it could be used to advantage.

For a passenger with a window seat above the wing, the sight of the deployment of these Flaps and Slats was astounding—the wing would seem to spread like an eagle's with one able to see right through the middle. As Boeing says, it was these sophisticated, triple-slotted trailing edge flaps and new leading edge Slats that gave the 727 low-speed landing and takeoff performance unprecedented for a commercial jet, allowing it to be accommodated by smaller airports than those the 707 required. Its fuselage width was nevertheless the same as that of the 707.

The operational flexibility these flaps and slats provided was much appreciated by pilots, but at the beginning, they did not also realize that they presented a danger. Extremely high sink rates could develop without them noticing—it required 37% thrust just to maintain level flight with full flap. Recovery from a high sink rate, and especially at low airspeeds, takes time; and in the early days, there were occasions when there was not enough with disastrous results.

Other novel features that made it possible to deploy the 727 at smaller airports with limited facilities were

- An auxiliary power unit (APU) providing electrical power without having to run the engines.
- The ability to back up without a tractor.
- An underbelly gravity-operated airstair enabling passengers to embark and disembark without provision of steps by the airport.
  This airstair was famously deployed mid-flight by a hijacker to parachute from the aircraft with $200,000 in ransom money. See D. B. Cooper.

There was one incident in 1979 involving the 727 (not included in *Air Crashes and Miracle Landings*), where a 727 climbed to 39,000 ft to escape from a 100 M.P.H. headwind that had been delaying progress and using up their fuel. At that exceptionally high altitude, the aircraft suddenly yawed, flipped over and entered a precipitous dive. Deployment of the Spoilers/Air Brakes had no effect, and it was only by lowering the Landing Gear (Undercarriage) at airspeeds where doing so would normally be unthinkable (with the result that the housing was ripped off) that the captain, a Captain Gibson, was able to recover.

Though many thought Gibson a hero, the authorities accused him, the copilot and engineer of having intentionally deployed the slats to be able to fly better at that great height—it being alleged that pilots were in the habit of doing this surreptitiously. Gibson always maintained that one of the slats had deployed on its own with no input from the crew.

An excellent account of this muddied affair can be found in Stanley Stewart's *Emergency—Crisis on the Flight Deck.* According to Stewart, deploying the slats did not improve performance at great heights and the whole idea of pilots doing this on a large scale must therefore have been largely untrue.

Whatever the facts, it was an early demonstration of how dangerous it can be if something untoward happens when cruising at very great heights, as in the case of Air France Flight AF447 lost not long ago on a flight between Rio de Janeiro and Paris. See Coffin Corner.

737 (Boeing 737) [1968] 6,000+

Boeing's 737 series is the most successful series of aircraft ever, having passed through 3-generations, and still going strong. The number produced, and on order, exceeds 7,000.

It is a narrow body twinjet, especially favored by low-cost carriers such as the U.S.'s Southwest Airlines and Ireland's Ryanair. When first conceived in the mid 1960s, the aircraft had relatively small Pratt & Whitney JT8D-1 engines under the wings allowing the aircraft to sit very close to the ground. This had a number of advantages such as facilitating servicing of the engines. It also meant faster turn round times as baggage, victuals and so on did not have to be raised high up in the air. One disadvantage of having the engines so close to the ground was ingestion of sand and dirt from unpaved runways, but now most of these have now been paved over. A greater problem has been lack of room for more powerful larger diameter engines. The solution chosen was to place engine accessories to the side of the engines, which explains the odd-looking oval-shaped nacelles.

Bean- counting (or the desire to reduce certification or pilot retraining costs through commonality) in the domain of cockpit instrumentation has very likely been a factor, though not the primary cause, in some silly accidents. These pale in impact when viewed against the total number of aircraft sold. See Grandfathering.

747 (Boeing 747 Classic and variants) [1970] 1,500+

This was the second *betting-the-company* airliner project for Boeing, and represented a much greater risk than the 707, even though again based on the design for a military aircraft. The military aircraft was to be a freighter (cancelled in the early stages) able to be loaded from the front as well as from the rear, hence the perching of the flight deck of the 747 so high above the ground.

The airliner that resulted from this was a quantum jump in size over existing ones, and resulted in teething troubles, and notably the flexing of the exceptionally large-diameter engines. Some joked that some early versions of the 747 were actually five-engine craft, as they might have an extra pylon to carry a spare engine. Even the inaugural Pan Am commercial flight from New York to London on January 1, 1970 was less than a total success. From memory, the author remembers a journalist saying something along the lines

> *The jumbo revved up its engines at the end of the runway for takeoff, only to have to limp back to the terminal like a wounded beast.*

The 747 went on to become one of the most successful aircraft ever, opening long-distance air travel to the wider public. With no direct competition, it was a great source of income for Boeing, and some assert that the profits on the 747 enabled the company to offer keener prices for its smaller aircraft where there was real competition.

It was again Juan Trippe, the head of Pan Am, who played a crucial role. He not only persuaded Boeing to go ahead with the project in the first place, but also later in persuaded the then U.S. President Johnson that even in an economic downturn it made sense to keep alive a project that would open up long distance air travel to the masses.

747-8 (Boeing 747-8) [2010?]

When Airbus came up with their super-jumbo A380 which threatened the position of the 747, Boeing at first said times had changed and market research showed passengers now prefer to fly point-to-point rather than via hubs, and that by implication a giant aircraft no longer looked viable.

Perhaps to avoid Airbus having the clear run pricewise they had enjoyed with the 747, and perhaps more importantly because they thought that without the development costs associated with a complete new design, they could produce an aircraft to compete relatively cheaply, Boeing decided to offer a super-stretched version of the 747. Using some of the technology developed for the 787 Dreamliner, it would have improved performance, and be called the 747-8. Both the airliner and the freighter versions would involve a stretch of 5.6 m (18.3 ft) over the 747-400 versions.

Things have not gone smoothly with a number of problems and production delays. Recently, the U.K.'s *Flight International* editorialized that

Boeing's problems with the super-stretched 747-8, parallel those with first 747s in that both programs were starved of engineering resources in favor of prestige projects. In the case of the first 747, it was the subsequently cancelled *Supersonic Transport*; in the case of the 747-8, it has been the *787-Dreamliner*.

Another reason for the starving of resources in the case of the 748-8 may have been the lack of enthusiasm initially shown by the airlines, with Lufthansa being the only one to place launch orders for the passenger version. The freighter version has fared somewhat better, partly because Airbus has had to postpone production of the freighter version of the A380 to concentrate resources on the delayed passenger version.

The aircraft will use the General Electric GEnx-2B next generation turbofan engine designed for medium-capacity long-haul aircraft, a version of which will also power the Boeing 787 Dreamliner.

757 (Boeing 757) [1983] 1,050

Reflecting the enhanced reliability and power of jet engines, the Boeing 757 medium range twinjet was designed to replace the very successful 727 trijet. Avionics, controls and handling were to be similar to those of the larger Boeing 767 being developed around the same time, so pilots could easily switch from one to the other without special type approval.

The British government and Rolls Royce had tried to have the wings made in Britain, and while they failed to do so, the U.K.'s Rolls Royce supplied the engines used initially and remained a serious player. While a very successful aircraft, its sales were largely in the Americas.

Like its elder brother, the 757, the 757 featured in Nine-Eleven as

- the aircraft that was crashed into the Pentagon with the loss of 125 lives on the ground and 64 (including 5 hijackers) on board

- and, the aircraft that was crashed into open country with the loss of 44 on board (including 4 hijackers) after the passengers confronted the hijackers.

The Peruvian airliner that flew into the sea after an aircraft cleaner had left masking tape over the Pitot Probes was also a 757. See *Air Crashes and Miracle Landings.*

767 (Boeing 767) [1982] 1,000+

The Boeing 767 wide-body twinjet has the distinction of being involved in a number of famous and infamous incidents. This is largely because this rather commonplace medium- to long-haul aircraft has been in such wide use on relatively long haul flights.

- Two 767s laden with fuel for transcontinental flights were intentionally flown into the north and south towers of the World Trade Center in New York on Nine-Eleven.

- An Ethiopian Airlines 767 ran out of fuel after being hijacked forcing the pilot to ditch it in the Indian Ocean in full view of bathers on a beach in near Comoros. Often cited in the media connection with the ditching of an Airbus in the Hudson River to show how difficult ditching an aircraft can be. There were survivors, and those that did not survive included some who inflated their life-vests prematurely and were unable to get out when the fuselage filled with water.

- EgyptAir Flight 990, a 767, crashed into the Atlantic Ocean some time after departing New York's JFK for Cairo. After analyzing the cockpit voice recordings and other evidence, the NTSB investigators concluded the first officer deliberately crashed the aircraft. The Egyptian side disputed this with the NTSB saying it was an example of a case where cockpit VIDEO recorder evidence would have been invaluable.

- An Air Canada 767 ran out of fuel after confusion over metric conversion coupled with fuel indication problems and managed to glide a considerable distance to land safely at a tiny Gimli airfield known to the copilot from his military service. Referred to as the *Gimli Glider* incident.

- Apart from a couple of incidents due to bad weather, there was one freakish incident where the left engine thrust reverser on a Lauda Air 767 suddenly deployed while the aircraft was over Thailand, causing it to crash with all 223 persons on board losing their lives.

Recently, Boeing based a bid for the next U.S. Air Force in-flight refueling platform on the 767 only to be beaten by a bid by Northrop-Grumman based on the Airbus A330, much to the chagrin of many in the U.S.

Boeing, not wanting to lose such as vast order that they thought was almost their right having supplied the previous platform, cried foul, and with political and other pressure managed to have the decision rejected. Now that the bidding rules have been revised making Boeing's position almost impregnable, the previous winners for a time declined to bid.

While not in the same class as regards size as the Boeing 747, air traffic controllers usually class the 767 as "heavy" in view of the nasty wake-turbulence it produces.

777 (Boeing 777) [1995] 860 as of April 2010

Seating more than 300 passengers the 777 is a long-range twinjet that has been remarkably successful, and whose sales have eaten into those of the

747. It was Boeing's first fly-by-wire airliner and is notable for having the largest diameter turbofan engines of any airliner.

Originally, Boeing was thinking of a 767 stretch, but, including for the first time in the design process a number of major airlines, came up with a new airliner with a wider diameter cabin than first envisaged. It was the first airliner to be certified for ETOPS operations right from the beginning, and owes much of its commercial success to fact that twin-engine airliners were being allowed to fly oceanic routes as much as 3-hours flying time from a diversion airfield. It holds the record for long-distance airliner flights, once held by the Airbus 340 with four engines. However, with two engines being cheaper to operate and maintain, the new ETOPS regulations nullified the A340's long-range oceanic advantage.

New airliners, such as variants of Boeing's own 787 Dreamliner and the projected Airbus A350 XWB threaten the 777 primacy on certain routes; so much so that Boeing is considering a replacement.

787 (Boeing 787—Dreamliner)

This is the prestige project mentioned above, with novel features both as regards methods of production and design.

It is Boeing's latest airliner with novel features such as using composites for the fuselage itself (rather than only for tail fins etc.). Another progressive feature is to use air pumped directly in from outside, instead of bleed air from the engines, for cabin pressurization, and to have the cabin pressurized at a more comfortable 6,000 ft rather than the customary 7,000-8,000 ft..

Yet another feature was Boeing's plan to outsource much of the production with outside companies delivering finished sections and parts for final assembly at Boeing's plant. This has not worked as well as hoped, with the problems being compounded by a shortage of fasteners and a lengthy strike by workers opposed to outsourcing.

These consequential delays coupled with the fact that Boeing had been very optimistic, some would say overoptimistic, regarding the production and testing scheduling, has meant that deliveries will be much later than promised, with Boeing having to pay compensation and offer leases on other aircraft such as the 767 and 777 to fill the gap.

9/11: Nine-Eleven (Hijacked airliners flown into WTC and Pentagon)

Shorthand for the climactic events of September 11, 2001 in the U.S. in which four aircraft were hijacked, two being flown intentionally into the World Trade Center in New York and one into the Pentagon. The fourth crashed (or was purposely crashed after a passenger uprising) in open country before reaching its target which could have been the U.S. Capitol building or the White House.

In the U.S., numerical dates have the month rather than the day first. Did the London Bombers choose July 7, 2005 (7/7), so that there would be no problem over this?

90 seconds (emergency evacuation)

For certification of an aircraft by the authorities, the manufacturer must prove (by tests with actual people) that evacuation is possible in 90 seconds. This is largely because aircraft fuselages although very strong are credit card thin and thus only be certain to be able to withstand a powerful external fire for 90 seconds.

Passengers often find it difficult to resist taking their cabin baggage with them—when an Air France Airbus caught fire after overrunning the runway on landing at Montreal, all survived despite many carrying their hand baggage.

Airlines should perhaps tell passengers to have essential medication on their person, and that anyone bringing hand luggage out with them in the course of an emergency evacuation will have it confiscated and even be punished for endangering the lives of others.

FAA regulations regarding who should be allowed to sit in (and allow themselves to be sat in) emergency exit rows appear very strict, and include a long list of physical, verbal, intellectual and linguistic abilities likely needed to open the door in an emergency, follow the crew's instructions and advise fellow passengers. For instance, the regulations say the person must be 15 years or older, be able to read the safety instructions and not have other responsibilities such as looking after young children, and not require a seat-belt extension.

One cannot say how this squares with Air France's intention to charge extra for those seats—often especially sought by those with long legs and the like.

The U.K.'s *Flight International* has recently dedicated special articles to the subject of evacuation. They maintain a rethink is needed, that current test methods using relatively fit individuals do not represent reality and that more use of computers should be made to simulate evacuation scenarios.

A300 (Airbus A300) [1974] 561

The A-300 was the first twin-engine wide-body airliner, and although sales were slow at the beginning, leading to many doubters, it eventually proved a great success as the increasing reliability of engines made the twin-engine design so viable besides being economical.

With the first wide-body, the four-engine Boeing 747 at the top of the market, and then the three-engine McDonnell Douglas DC-10 and Lockheed TriStar L1011 fighting it out just below without enough room for all three, the A300 was filling a niche.

The first flight was in 1972 and it entered commercial service a year and a half later in 1974. It was only from 1978 onwards that sales really began to improve. Many of the earlier sales had been arm-twisting sales where the French and German governments urged their national airlines to purchase the aircraft. Though sales never soared, the aircraft had a number of advanced features and became a steady seller. Altogether 561 units had been produced when production ceased in 2007.

An early decision to opt for U.S. General Electric CFM engines instead of a Rolls Royce engine still under development made it possible to put the aircraft into production earlier besides facilitating sales to the U.S.

Pratt and Whitney engines later became an option.

The decision to forgo the Rolls Royce engine infuriated the British Government. It is ironical that much of the success of the A300 can be attributed to the wings designed and manufactured by the British company Hawker-Siddeley, which the British Government was hoping would tie up with Boeing instead on similar work. Had Boeing been willing to make Hawker-Siddeley more of an equal partner, rather than a subcontractor shouldering considerable risk but little chance of participating in any success, the A300 and subsequent Airbus aircraft might never have been the success they were.

A320 (Airbus A320 family) [1988] 4,254+

The A320 family includes the smaller A319 and even smaller A318, and the larger A321.

The A320 and variants have proved very successful with the aircraft still in production, with a decision on a re-engined version imminent, so that its life can be extended until a technology evolves enough for a completely new design to be worthwhile.

A330 (Airbus A330) [1994] 680+

A340 (Airbus A340) [1993] 370+

The two aircraft have many structural parts in common, the main difference being that the A340 has four engines, whereas the A330 has two. Having the possibility of having four engines or two seemed to have been a clever idea, but much less so now that ETOPS certified twin-engine airliners are allowed to fly over oceans two or even three hours flying time from the nearest possible landing place. As a result, the Boeing 777 has eaten into the A340's potential sales, and with sales now sluggish, it is likely to give way to the A350.

Before the Boeing 777-LR, the A340-500 was the airliner with the longest range and was used by Singapore Airlines for the world's longest scheduled flight of 18 ½ hours between Singapore and New York. Until the arrival of the stretched Boeing 747-8, the A340 held the record for being the longest commercial aircraft in the world.

A350 (Airbus A350)

Airbus with their planned A350, as direct competitor to the Boeing 787, are playing catch-up, and might benefit technically (though not commercially) by being second—reminiscent of Boeing playing second fiddle with their 707 to the British de Havilland Comet, the world's first jetliner. Improved techniques for evaluating the performance of materials mean that the Boeing 787 is unlikely to suffer a fate similar to that of the first Comets.

A380 (Airbus 380) [2007] 40+

The super-jumbo fully twin-deck airbus now in regular commercial service after delays, mainly due to a discrepancy in software programs used for wiring at two different production locations.

Launch customers were Singapore Airlines (with 12 First Class 'suites'), Emirates (with two 5-minute showers in First Class and a bar for First and Business at the rear of the upper deck), and Qantas. All three airlines have put the accent on space, comfort and facilities for their premium passengers, rather than on maximizing total number of seats. The aircraft is proving very popular with passengers, but the airlines mentioned have some reservations about delayed departures and even cancellations of flights due to the sophisticated, some allege over-sophisticated, computer software identifying non-existent faults.

Despite continuing production problems, Airbus and its owner, EADS, is increasingly optimistic, thanks in great part to the faith placed in the A380 by Emirates, who have added to their already very significant orders. See Connectors.

Facts and figures

Maximum Ramp Weight:	562t
Maximum Take-off Weight	560t
Maximum Landing Weight	386t
Maximum Zero Fuel Weight	361t
Maximum Fuel Capacity	310 thousand liters

According to the *Financial Times* (German Edition) the cost of the A380 was 251.6m Euros ($316m; £173.1m) in June 2006.

A truly remarkable moving panoramic view of the A380 cockpit can be seen at http://www.gillesvidal.com/blogpano/cockpit1.htm

AAIB: Air Accident Investigation Branch

Conducts air accident investigations in the U.K.

Abort

Cancel something one was about to do or in the process of doing, such as a taking off or landing.

a/c: aircraft

ACARS: Aircraft Communications Addressing and Reporting System

Something that has been around for some time, but that has only come to the fore in the media in connection with the crash of the Air France A330 that crashed in the South Atlantic en route from Rio de Janeiro to Paris.

A somewhat novel feature of this disaster was that automated messages sent by via satellite for maintenance purposes rather than digital data recorders and cockpit voice recorders might prove the key to finding out what happened.

The ACARS system has three functions

- Providing a pilot-controller data link
- Exchanging operational information with the airline.

  This can include automatic reporting of position and say the moment the nose wheel leaves the ground on takeoff. For instance, United Airlines would have used this feature on 9/11 when warning, to no avail, Flight 93 about *cockpit intrusions.*

- Maintenance data download

  Previously maintenance staff had to access the Quick Access Data Recording on the aircraft's arrival to find out how the engines and other equipment had been behaving and what special servicing is needed. Now, with ACARS, they can be ready with the necessary staff and spare parts, and this is perhaps the reason why the system is now so widely used.

Following this AF447 crash, there have been suggestions that this system should replace or complement the "black boxes". Eventually this should be possible but now there are bandwidth problems and problems of cost, especially where use of satellites is involved.

Accelerate-Stop Distance

Calculated overall distance required to accelerate from commencement of take off to take off decision speed (V_1), abort take-off, and brake safely to a halt.

Accident Models (Academic Theories)

Academic work on the probability (inevitability), causes and avoidance of accidents is very extensive with great contributions by psychologists and academics concerned with the safety implications of nuclear power plants.

Dozens if not hundreds of books can be found on the subject which can seem so simple at some levels and so complex at others.

Though not for the faint hearted, Wiegmann and Shappell's A Human Error Approach to Aviation Accident Analysis published by Ashgate, explains how various academics have treated the subject.

See Swiss Cheese Model and Normal Accident.

ADC: Air Data Computer

It simply means a computer handling data regarding the air with which the aircraft is in contact, and in particular, the **static** pressure, which is the actual pressure at that height, and the Pitot pressure, which is the extra pressure produced when airflow enters a forwards facing port. By comparing the two, it can calculate the aircraft's airspeed.

The ADC also calculates barometric height (altitude), vertical speed (climb/sink rate), air temperature and Mach number.

ADF: Automatic Direction Finder

Equipment that determines the direction of a radio transmitter.

Can be tuned to a NDB (Non Directional Beacon) or even to an AM radio station and therefore not limited to line-of-sight broadcasting stations, as would be the case with FM. Can be set in two modes

- Needle pointing to transmitter relative to nose of aircraft
- Needle pointing relative to magnetic North.

Administration or Agency? (U.S. usage)

Non-U.S. journalists should be aware that the *A* at the end of the acronyms for some well-known U.S. organizations might well stand for Administration and not Agency.

Notable examples are

- NASA — National Aeronautics and Space Administration
- TSA — Transportation Security Administration
- FAA — Federal Aviation Administration

Exceptions are

- CIA — Central Intelligence Agency
- NSA — National Security Agency
- FEMA — Federal Emergency Management Agency

Incidentally, TSA and FEMA are part of the DHS (Department of Homeland Security) created in the aftermath of 9/11.

ADS-B: Automatic Dependent Service-Broadcast

The technology expected to be at the heart of future more efficient air traffic control systems. See NextGen.

The principal is that the aircraft automatically broadcasts a whole range of information—far exceeding that *squawked* by the traditional Transponder—and notably

- Its exact position (determined by GPS and crosschecked with other navigational instruments)
- Height, **ground**speed and airspeed

- Climb or Sink Rate, Rate and Direction of Turn or absence thereof
- Control inputs: Say prior knowledge of advance of throttle levers—actual acceleration can take several seconds from idle detent.

  Of course, traditional info given out by airliner transponders such as identity, squawk code and so on would be included.

This information would be shown on air traffic controllers monitors and on monitors on other aircraft within a radius of some 150 miles. Furthermore, traffic warning and collision avoidance systems (TCAS) would operate more effectively since they would take into account action already being taken by the respective aircraft. In addition, such a system would lessen the risk of any collision scenario developing in the first place.

The use of the word *dependent* in the name may seem strange, but merely means that from the air traffic controllers' point of view, the info regarding position and so on depends entirely on what he or she is being told by the equipment on the aircraft and not what his or her radar sees *with its own eyes*. The controllers would also have their traditional *independent* radar monitors.

Purported advantages

- Greater accuracy would allow aircraft to be closer together and hence more efficient use of airspace
- Works in the absence of radar coverage, such as in isolated areas or in the lee of mountains
- Often possible to preclude potential conflicts
- Functions also on the ground, even indicating when an aircraft is *just moving off* or a runway incursion is *about* to occur. It would have prevented the worst-ever aviation disaster where two 747s collided on Tenerife
- Other features such as weather depiction and advisories can be incorporated in the ADS-B data link;
- Aircraft would save time and fuel by flying more direct routes rather than the traditional airways between radio beacons.

Objections voiced by opponents

- Some opponents claim that terrorists might exploit the information an aircraft transmits regarding its position to destroy it, say by flying a model plane or GA aircraft into it. Advocates counter this by saying there are simpler ways, such as shoulder launched SAMs, to bring down an aircraft near an airport.

See Aircraft-Centric.

14

Aerodynamics Index (NASA Glenn Research Center)

http://www.grc.nasa.gov/WWW/K-12/VirtualAero/BottleRocket/airplane/short.html

This is an amazingly comprehensive online site entitled: *Beginners Guide to Aerodynamics*.

Although described as being for *beginners*, they mean dedicated students. Perhaps conscious of this, a means of accessing the site according to ones knowledge level has now been incorporated. See Fallacies.

Aeroelasticity

Airfoils (Aerofoils), turbine blades and even bridges are not completely rigid and deform under the inertial, aerodynamic and elastic forces imposed on them or produced in them due to resulting harmonic oscillations. While this phenomenon can have harmful effects, it can sometimes be used to advantage.

Aerophile

An aviation buff (fan).

Aerotoxic Alliance (Association)

Tristan Loraine, of the U.K.'s Global Cabin Air Quality Executive, which campaigns for better cabin air quality, has said

> *The 146 is poorly designed, so the problem is particularly acute with that aircraft. I am not surprised Flybe staff are refusing to fly.*

AFCS: Automatic Flight Control System

Also IFCS: Integrated Flight Control System

Age of Pilot (maximum)

Maximum permitted age for commercial airline pilots varies from country to country. With older people who have looked after themselves—as airline pilots normally do—nowadays living longer, there has been a move to allow older pilots, even in the U.S., to work to 65 rather than 60.

This is something of a contentious issue at the airlines, not so much on safety grounds—there should always be a **younger** copilot to take charge in the event of the older man falling ill—but because of the differing financial according to the situation of the pilot concerned.

With so much at airlines based on seniority rather than ability, junior pilots do not want to see captains staying on as seat blockers. While senior pilots with advantageous pension plans are happy to retire early, those not so endowed, want to continue. In France, the government has been thinking of forcing through legislation to raise the age limit from 60 to 65 in the face of the threat of strike action by some pilots.

While the major airlines may be good at weeding out those whose faculties deteriorate with age, it is worth noting an article by Patrick R. Veillette Ph.D. entitled *Tombstone Mentality* in *Aviation Week* of June 24,

2008. He consulted some one hundred business aviation colleagues to learn their concerns about near misses with light aircraft, contaminated runways, and so on.

As regards ageing, he says the following:

> *The ageing pilot population within certain segments of the business aviation industry gave serious concern to many. Colleagues who frequently fly with the over-60 group notice deterioration in important sensory, perceptual, cognitive and motor skills that are important to piloting. They have noticed changes to an ageing pilot's ability to learn, memory, tolerance to fatigue, sleeping habits, physical changes, and so forth.*

He adds that pairing of pilots to avoid two very old pilots being together is not properly thought out—a mistake the major airlines would be unlikely to make.

agl: above ground level

Abbreviation used to indicate the height above ground level as opposed to sea level, such as 5,000 ft agl.

AIDS: Aircraft Integrated Data System

Aileron

Together with the rudder and elevators, represent the traditional fundamental control surfaces. They consist of hinged rectangular cutouts along the rear of the wings inversely linked control-wise, so that when those on one wing go up (pushing it down), those on the opposite wing go down (pushing it up). The ailerons control the aircraft in the lateral plane, making it bank, so passengers do not feel they are falling inwards or flying outwards on a turn. See Coordinated Flight.

AIM (Aeronautical Information Manual)

Official Guide to Basic Flight Information and ATC Procedures issued by the FAA. Covers all aspects and very comprehensive.

Air China

Air China is China's flag carrier based in Beijing. Not to be confused with Taiwan's *China Airlines (CI)*. Having *CA* as the airline's code is not helpful in this respect.

Air Force One

An emotive word for Americans partly because of the dramas (including movies) built around it, and partly because of the awe associated with the Presidency.

Even though the call sign *Air Force One* was first used in the nineteen-fifties for the aircraft carrying the President of the United States, the Boeing 707 used by President Kennedy was the first actual aircraft to be so designated by the public, or rather the media. In fact there are two Air Force Ones to ensure one is always serviceable.

Special features on these modified Boeing 747-200s include a shower for the President, accommodation for himself/herself and family, a conference room, and quarters for the press, officials, and Secret Service. Naturally, high-tech defensive mechanisms and secure communication facilities are important features.

Air Marshalls

Although many countries do have security people on board their aircraft, the U.S. has taken the idea of having incognito armed marshals on board most seriously. Although the exact figure is classified, *U.S.A Today* has stated that following the events of Nine-Eleven the number of air marshals jumped from 33 to between 3,000 and 4,000. The publication went on to say this surge in numbers has meant lowered standards, and demoralization. Part of the problem in attracting the right personnel is that life as a permanent passenger cannot be glamorous or stimulating.

Air Rage

The term air rage conjures up images of individuals causing disruption. However, in India the air rage once involved passengers acting in a group with them becoming so frustrated at being kept for ages in a holding pattern they all rushed towards the cockpit to threaten the pilots—almost compromising the control of the aircraft due to the shift in center of gravity.

Just as there is statistically usually a doctor or vet on board to help cope with a medical emergency, there are often burly military types on hand willing to help subdue an unruly passenger. Subjugation must not get so out of hand that the individual succumbs; say due to strangulation, as happened in one case.

While a panicking passenger trying to open a door to get out may cause much concern, the pressure differential at height forcing the plug doors shut means they are impossible to open unless near the ground. A passenger trying to take over control of the aircraft is another matter. On a BA flight to Nairobi, a panicking man struggling with the pilot to *"save the aircraft"* was only overcome at the very last moment with the aircraft diving so precipitously it was in danger of breaking apart even before hitting the ground. Nowadays, the reinforced and locked cockpit doors installed after 9/11 lessen the likelihood of a crazed (fearful) passenger fighting the pilots for control of the aircraft.

Air Traffic Clearance

Permission from ATC notably, but not exclusively, to taxi, takeoff, land, climb, descend, or enter controlled airspace.

Air Traffic Control (ATC)

To avoid aircraft colliding, an air traffic control system is established whereby the aircraft are given instructions by radio regarding routes, height and so on.

Different sets of controllers handle the various stages of a flight

- **Ground Control** handling taxiing at the airport
- **Tower** handling takeoffs & landings
- **Departure Control** handling period between control by the tower and handover to the Air Route Traffic Control called a Center
- **Center** handling traffic using air routes in the region. For instance, there will be a Chicago Center, New York Center and so on. The aircraft is handed from center to center until they want to land, at which point they descend and are handed over to
- **Approach**, which handles them until handover to the **Tower** for the actual landing.

Air Traffic Control in many countries, including the U.S., is conceptually antiquated and having difficulty in coping with increasing traffic. New technologies (See ADS-B) should allow aircraft to fly closer together and on more direct routes compared with the traditional Airways between radio beacons.

Air Traffic Flow Management (ATFM)

A system depending largely on computers whereby departure and arrival times are adjusted according to the airport to which they are headed can cope and to prevent aircraft arriving simultaneously and having to burn up fuel holding. See Departure—effect of late arrival of passenger(s) at gate.

Air Transport Association (ATA) [U.S.]

Washington-based lobbying group for the airline industry.

Allegedly, recently tried to divert passenger outrage at long delays by blaming corporate jets. In fact, though corporate jets have equal rights to the airlines as regards taking off and so on, on a first-come-first-served basis, they usually use different airports.

Underlying this dispute is a larger one, namely that according to the FAA's own estimates, private (GA) planes, which include both corporate jets and weekend fliers, account for 16 percent of the air traffic control system's overhead but contribute only 3 percent of the fees earmarked to run it. At major U.S. airports corporate jets pay next to nothing compared with an airliner.

Air Transport World: ATW

Trade magazine for the aviation industry with "daily news" on website and via email. Based in Maryland, U.S.A, with offices around the world. Even has a section in Chinese.

Exceptionally clean website: http://www.atwonline.com/

Airbags

News that certain airlines such as Singapore Airlines are equipping First and Business seats in a given aircraft such as a new Boeing-777 with airbags may seem discriminatory. However, according to the only FAA certified U.S. manufacturer, Phoenix-based *Amsafe Aviation*, this is only because premium seats have more protruding places where occupants are liable to bang their heads.

Talking about airbags and seats in general, an Air Canada spokesperson has said airbags were installed in seats failing to meet the government's "head strike criteria". (i.e. *The seats might be too near a bulkhead or a wall in the front row.*)

Unlike airbags in cars, that spring towards the occupant, aircraft airbags are usually integrated into the seatbelt and come up between the passenger and the seat or bulkhead in front.

Air France and Cathay Pacific intend to extend their use to Economy Class. This is partly because the airlines use a particular type of hard shell seat, all aircraft built in the U.S. from October 2010 must conform to standards designed to keep passengers conscious through an impact involving deceleration at 16 times the force of gravity so that they can escape any subsequent fire. (By the end of 2011, the European Aviation Safety Agency will apply similar rules.) According to the June 2011 Bloomberg article on the subject, the devices cost about $1,200 apiece, versus $25 for a regular seatbelt.

Airbus

> This manufacturer's entry is very long as it aims to throw light on the situations that all Airframers faced, both historically and more recently. The entry for Boeing is very much shorter as its much longer history is covered via the entries for individual Boeing aircraft.

At the turn of the Millennium, Airbus was snapping at Boeing's heels with sales reaching 50% of the market. It seemed that Boeing had become complacent, set in its ways, and unable to put a foot right. Then as Boeing was regaining its feet by offering of the 787 Dreamliner, it was to be the turn of Airbus to stumble.

1. The Beginnings

When the idea of a European Airbus twin-engine wide-body aircraft was first seriously floated in the late sixties, there was much confusion and lack of coherence regarding what airliners should be developed, in both Europe and the U.S.

Commentators have made much of the fact that worthy British airliners such as the Trident and the Vickers VC-10 were commercial failures because the manufacturers specked their aircraft according to the requirements of British airlines. In the case of the Trident, the original speck, which happened to coincide with what airlines in the U.S. finally decided they needed, was downsized to suit British European Airways (BEA) flying short routes to European destinations. In the second case, the VC-10 was over-specked as regards performance for British Overseas Airways Corporation (BOAC) flying long routes via airports with poor runways and hot climates where engines perform badly. This resulted in an aircraft with a reputation for being fuel-hungry, and killed its prospects on routes where even a 2% extra fuel burn was significant to airlines other than BOAC. The countries en route shortly afterwards upgraded their airports making the over-speck unnecessary.

U.S. manufacturers similarly made the mistake of trying to satisfy everyone including the relatively few that needed a trijet to be able to fly routes over the sea. As a result, they built two tri-jets at a time when three engines were mandatory for oversea routes. This mistake of building two tri-jets with insufficient market provided the opening that the Europeans needed. Had that not been the case, the launch of the Airbus, the world's first twin-aisle twin-engine wide-body would have been even more difficult than it was.

According to John Newhouse's *The Sporty Game*, 1966 was a key year. This was not only because of the agreement between Boeing and Pan American regarding the 747, but also because it was the year that Frank Kolk of American Airlines sent Boeing, Douglas, and Lockheed the specifications of a new airliner, much smaller than the 747 that would best fit his company's forecast growth in passenger traffic. He called it the Jumbo Twin, a double-aisle wide-body double-aisle aircraft capable of carrying as many as 250 passengers a distance of 2,100 miles at subsonic speed.

This encouraged Lockheed and McDonnell Douglas to pursue their wide-body ventures—but for the reasons mentioned above with three engines. This allowed the Europeans to go ahead with their aircraft, along the lines proposed by Kolk. Frenchman Beteille, who was the mastermind of the Airbus project at the time, is said to have said Kolk's list of requirements represented a significant input to the Airbus project.

Though difficult to believe now, the Airbus was not getting most of the French government funds allotted to aviation. Those were going to the supersonic Concorde much favored by President de Gaulle's as means of enhancing France's prestige. This impeded the Airbus project, though

Airbus staffers claim technology developed for the Concorde project contributed to subsequent Airbus projects such as the A320. Here again, things across the Pond were not as they subsequently seemed, as this prompted the Americans to pursue studies of a possible supersonic airliner so as not to be left behind by the Europeans, and this meant that the Boeing 747 and other projects were also for a time starved of resources.

Meanwhile the Germans resolutely refused to support the Concorde project, deeming it unlikely to succeed commercially. On the other hand, they supported an airbus type project, but mainly financially as their aircraft-manufacturing base was then so limited.

2. Britain's Hesitant Role

Before and during the conception of the A300 Airbus, the British government had been hoping that Hawker Siddeley would collaborate with U.S. companies, such as Lockheed working on the TriStar. However, on realizing they would be merely be a junior subcontractor, Hawker Siddeley decided to go with Airbus, encouraged by the fact that the father of the project, Roger Béteille, had great admiration for their expertise in wing design and work on the Trident.

Hawker Siddeley invested their own funds on tooling for the project, with a subsequent loan from the Germans who had increased their share when the British government pulled out fearing they would never recoup their investment. Incidentally, Rolls Royce, whom the British government had saved from bankruptcy being brought about by the costs incurred in developing the RB-211 engine for the Lockheed TriStar, was able to provide the Rolls-Royce RB207 engine at little extra research cost, thus making the project as a whole much easier to realize financially.

In 1977 Hawker Siddeley became part of British Aerospace, which in January 1979 took up a 20% share in Airbus Industrie. (Recently, on deciding that its future lay in working with the U.S., British Aerospace relinquished this share, with some argument, as the value of its shares had fallen in the light of revelations regarding the problems associated with the production of the A380 superjumbo.) The wing-making facility at near Bristol in the U.K. was bought by GKN, so that aspect is still in British hands.

3. The A320 Paves the Way to Success and Overconfidence

The A300 was innovative in that it was the first wide-body twin-aisle twin-engine airliner. However, sales were sluggish at the beginning, and it was only in later years that they picked, making a good total in aggregate. See A300.

It was the technically innovative A320 fly-by-wire single-aisle narrow-body short- to medium-range airliner that placed Airbus in the Major League, with many orders even before the first commercial flight. Though it went on to be, and still is, a great commercial success, there were several crashes in the early days—described in *Air Crashes and Miracle Landings.*

The first was a ridiculous one where the pilot of a brand new Air France A320 cut things too close while showing off at a tiny air show, and most others attributed to pilot error and their unfamiliarity with sophisticated computerized systems.

While there is no space here to go into the twists and turns of the Airbus saga, the fact that Airbus performed as well as it did up until the development of the Airbus superjumbo, A380, is something of a wonder. That is considering the inherent inefficiencies of an organization with international partners and two countries vying for power via key personalities, all the time making sure the other could not become the key decision-maker.

4. "Humbled Airbus Learns Hard Lessons"

Those, including the present writer, witnessing the maiden flight of the A380 at Toulouse in southern France did not realize that some of the voluptuous maiden's inner garments had been left unbuttoned.

This was only made known much later when Airbus informed launch customers that their aircraft would be delayed, mainly due to problems with the wiring, which could not be connected on being found to be too short. The consequent fall in the value of Airbus shares just when British Aerospace was exercising its option to sell them back angered BAE. There were also accusations of insider trading by senior people at Airbus in the know.

Nicola Clark, an *International Herald Tribune* Reporter, and aviation and transportation journalist, based in Paris whose articles also appear in the New York Times has studied the affair in depth and written a detailed prize-winning article entitled *A Humbled Airbus Learns Hard Lessons*. Published as early as December 14, 2006, she tells how when some 200 German technicians came to Toulouse with hundreds of kilometers of electric wire to thread painstakingly through the rear and front fuselages sections made in Hamburg they found an unexpected problem. After sometimes following very labyrinthine paths, there was often not enough wire left for them to reach the corresponding connectors in adjacent sections.

The technicians pointed this out but management did not take their views seriously perhaps because problems were to be expected in so complex an aircraft. Later senior management was too occupied with political and territorial infighting to give the problem the attention it needed. According to Clark, obfuscation and failure to deal with the problem early on was to prove very costly. How had such a situation arisen in the first place?

Almost unbelievably, according to Nicola Clark, the problem costing billions of dollars had apparently arisen because the Germans had insisted on using an out of date American 2-D program for the wiring layout while the French were using a better 3-D program. Clark suggests that it was not just a question of German pride and avoiding the costly nuisance of changing to another program, but also the fact that the less efficient 2-D program required more workers and would boost employment there. She was not able to get an answer on this from union representatives.

Airbus said the problem had simply arisen from use of *incompatible* software, which probably glosses over the fact that in reality the complexity of the paths the wires followed meant that the German 2-D program was underestimating the length of wire needed for it to reach the specified point (connector) on the adjacent section of the fuselage. Now it seems Airbus has even unsure of its 3-D program and to be entirely sure is using a wooden mock-up to simulate the paths of the wiring.

Airbus, now owned by EADS, is weathering both these problems and those arising from the problematic A400 military transport contract partly thanks to the cushioning provided by the good order book for other aircraft. There seems to be more transparency and openness, but dealing with unions in different countries while rationalizing is not proving easy.

It is interesting to note that Boeing had it own problems with the 787 Dreamliner. While of lesser magnitude, similar obfuscation and promising a too tight production schedule on a highly complex project similarly compounded Boeing's problems.

In mid-2010, Airbus indicated that sales of the A380 were beginning to revive and prospects were improving. Emirates added a firm order for an extra 32, bringing its total order to 90 for the superjumbo. To the amazement of many, the airline intimated that might not be the last. Interestingly, China is seen by Airbus as a market likely to require a large number of superjumbos, though Hong Kong's Cathay Pacific's failure to purchase the A380 has been something of a setback. The airline had participated in discussions at the initial planning stage.

Aircraft

In civil aviation circles, calling an airliner a *plane, aeroplane* (U.K.) or *airplane* (U.S. & Canada) is frowned upon. One definition of *aircraft* is any machine supported in some manner by the surrounding air—thus rockets, which do not depend on movement through the air to stay aloft, are not aircraft. There are two categories of aircraft

- Craft that are lighter than air such as airships (called *aerostats*)
- Craft that are heavier than air (called *aerodynes*)

In the media, unmanned aircraft are often referred to as *drones,* but are now officially increasingly called RPVs (Remotely Piloted Vehicles) or UAVs (Unmanned Aerial Vehicles).

Aircraft Registration Codes

Except for a few countries (such as **G** for Great Britain, **I** for Italy, **D** for Germany, **RA** for Russian Federation and **JA** for Japan), the code prefixes on aircraft denoting their country of registration are not immediately obvious. Note that U.S.-registered aircraft start with the letter **N**, while those registered in China begin with **B** with further letters or an additional number being subcategories for Hong Kong, Macau, and Taiwan.

See http://en.wikipedia.org/wiki/Aircraft_registration, FAA and other sites.

Aircushion Seats

Some premium seats now use aircushions, which have the advantages over foam in that they can be rendered soft when the seat is upright and hard when horizontal, besides saving a considerable amount of weight.

AirDisaster.Com. [http://www.airdisaster.com]

Website with much information and many photos relating to air accidents, the fear of flying, and so on.

Airfoil [U.S.] /Aerofoil [U.K.]

A wing, propeller blade, or similar, passing through air to provide lift; change of direction; or in the case of a propeller, forward force.

Airframe

Essentially, the aircraft structure minus the engines. A well-maintained airframe can be updated, and see its value increased, by installing the latest avionics making it easier and more pleasant to fly and even more fuel-efficient.

Airframer

Though the media refer to Airbus and Boeing as aircraft manufacturers, a more appropriate word increasingly used in the aviation business is *Airframer*, to distinguish them from engine-makers. Airframers make most of their profit when they sell an aircraft, whereas the engine makers may hardly make any profit at that point, and would sometimes be satisfied with no profit as the profits come from maintenance and parts—somewhat like what happens with some family cars.

Airline Codes

These are IATA codes used in flight numbers, etc.

See http://www.airlinecodes.co.uk/

Airline Deregulation Act (U.S.)

The Airline Deregulation Act passed by the U.S. Congress in 1978 gradually released the grip of the Civil Aeronautics Board on air travel in the U.S. Up until then, airfares had been regulated to allow the airlines a return of 12% on flights that were 55% full, and getting approval to fly a new route could take years, with the possibility that approval would be finally refused by the CAB.

Internationally, IATA would fix fares at high levels so that air travel was very much for the rich or people on business.

After 1978, there followed a period with the introduction of larger aircraft able to transport the masses, where charter flights were smashing prices and flag carriers were selling seats officially at full-price and unofficially through bucket shops at large discounts.

Airport Codes

Derivation of most codes is obvious. For example, LHR stands for London Heathrow.

See http://www.airlinecodes.co.uk/.

Aisle

Wide-body aircraft have two aisles and narrow-bodies a single aisle with passengers often sitting three-abreast on either side. Recently, an old proposal by McDonnell Douglas for a twin-aisle light twin has been considered. While two aisles would improve comfort, the main thinking behind this is that two aisles would decrease turnaround times since people can board and disembark much more quickly with two aisles. With a single aisle, it only takes one person to bring boarding to a halt.

Airspeed

Speed of aircraft through the air as opposed to groundspeed, and usually measured in knots.

Airspeed Indicator (ASI)

A key instrument indicating airspeed. In modern cockpits, airspeed is often shown in an easy-to-comprehend *tape* (band) alongside the artificial horizon as well as by the traditional dedicated air speed indicator.

Airway

Designated routes followed by aircraft. Usually marked by radio beacons (See VOR) when over land. Countries usually have two sets of airways with different designations according to their height. Some countries follow the U.S. system of designating the (lower) *Airways* as *Victor Airways* and the *Upper Air Routes* as *Jet routes* (say 18,000 ft and above)).

Airways are usually between VOR beacons with the pilot following the outbound radial and then the inbound radial of the next one, switching between the two once the latter's signal strength becomes superior—which is not necessarily half-way as VOR signal strengths vary.

Oceanic routes have a different nomenclature.

With the eventual introduction of GPS-based ADS-B, airways are likely to lose their importance as aircraft take routes that are more direct. However, they have proved their worth, and would have to be kept for use in the event of something going wrong with the satellite-based system.

Airworthiness Directive (AD)

Mandatory orders by authorities such as the FAA for rectification of a defect found after certification of the aircraft model. May be immediate, in which case the aircraft may not fly until the rectification has been effected, or mandatory within a certain time or number of flying hours, or even at the next time the aircraft is due for routine maintenance.

Greatly feared by airlines as such directives could ground a large part of their fleet at peak periods, and hence they will try to find ways to soften the stance of the authorities as in the case of the DC-10 cargo hold door mechanism where there was eventually a 'gentleman's agreement' with the FAA.

Alarp: as low as is reasonably practicable

Term for viewing *risk* in say the military domain where operational constraints mean the perfection sought in civil aviation is not practical. The term came to public notice in the course of the inquest into the lives of military personnel lost in the U.K.'s Nimrod (AWACS) disaster in Afghanistan.

Alcohol

Airlines have strict regulations concerning the consumption of alcohol by pilots before flying. Some say none within 8 hours, and others within 24 hours of flying. In the U.K., the legal limit for airline pilots is 20 micrograms of alcohol per 100 milliliters of breath, while for drivers (motorists) it is 35 micrograms of alcohol per 100 milliliters of breath. The occasional pilot arrested after a breath-test in the cockpit has usually been denounced by ground staff or passenger who had seen them drinking, or smelt drink on their breath.

Occasionally, pilots have been arrested way over the limit, but these do seem to be exceptions. Airlines have programs to try to detect crew with alcohol problems.

It has been pointed out that the dangers of fatigue represent a much greater risk. See NTSB's Most Wanted list.

See Drug Testing (Random).

Alerts

With onboard computers able to detect all sorts of problems, in addition to the traditional ones of being about to hit the ground or landing without lowering the undercarriage, pilots receive all sorts of aural and visual alerts. The problem with some alerts is pilots are liable to ignore them or even turn the warning systems off in the event of repeated spurious alerts.

An airline trying to introduce a system to prevent runway incursions in Alaska was faced with pilot opposition due to spurious alerts. Indeed, after having turned the system off, they subsequently narrowly averted an incident, which the system would have highlighted.

The *Mont St Odile* disaster years ago in France where a French Air Inter Airbus flew into a mountain might not have happened had the GPWS (Ground Proximity Warning System) not been deactivated for the same reason even though it was mandatory in the U.S. at the time.

Algorithm

A sophisticated-sounding word not easy to define and that is why it so handy. It is the series of instructions computers use to achieve an end (do something), solve a problem or simulate a set of circumstances. While a major computer program can be considered as a vast collection of algorithms, the term is usually used restrictively, such as saying *"Company X is developing better **algorithms** for predicting fan blade longevity in its new engine"*.

Alliance (Airline Alliance)

A constellation of airlines bound by agreements allowing passengers earning *Air Miles* and gaining executive club privileges on one (or several) to exploit those miles and privileges to various degrees on any one of them.

There are three main alliances comprising the following full members (Affiliates are not included)

THE STAR ALLIANCE

- Adria
- Air Canada
- Air China
- Air New Zealand
- ANA
- Asiana Airlines
- Austrian
- Blue1
- Bmi
- Brussels Airlines
- Continental Airlines
- Croatia Airlines
- Egyptair
- LOT
- Polish Airlines
- Lufthansa
- Scandinavian Airlines
- Shanghai Airlines
- Singapore Airlines
- South African Airways
- Spanair
- Swiss
- TAM
- TAP Portugal
- Thai
- Turkish Airlines
- United
- US Airways
- Air India (future member)

ONE WORLD

- American Airlines
- British Airways
- Cathay Pacific
- Finnair
- Iberia

- Japan Airlines
- Malèv
- Mexican
- Qantas
- Royal Jordanian

SKY TEAM

- Aeroflot
- Aeroméxico
- Air Europa
- Air France
- Alitalia
- China Southern
- Czech Airlines

- Delta
- Kenya Airways
- KLM
- Korean Air
- TAROM
- Vietnam Airlines

In July 2010, the *Wall Street Journal* had a very illuminating article by Scott McCartney, entitled *Shopping for Perks among the Big Airline Alliances*, suggesting that rather than choosing which airline to fly on, one should think in terms of which alliance to join. Of course, this really only applies to frequent flyers, and particularly those travelling at company expense on full fare Business Class or First Class tickets, where they can easily gain Elite or Gold status and earn Air Miles that can be used for personal advantage.

The *WSJ* pointed out that each alliance has its pros and cons, some with more cons than others, and the choice depends on the nature of the advantages sought—choice of destinations, ability to use air miles on other carriers in the alliance, and last but not least for many, the quality of the lounges and facilities provided.

The article pointed out that the Star Alliance besides being the largest alliance is the only one embracing several U.S. carriers. That One World, though smaller, has airlines proud of the facilities they offer for business people using the major business hubs (London, Hong Kong, Tokyo and New York). Sky Team is notable for having airlines that are the strongest in their particular regions, namely having Delta, the largest carrier in the U.S., and Air France-KLM, the largest in Europe.

Readers should refer to the article in question as some members opt out regarding particular advantages. However, in general, the Star Alliance is the best for upgrades using air miles, and One World is best for lounge access. For those wanting to redeem air miles in exchange for tickets to most places in the world, the Star Alliance is again best.

Alpha-floor (Airbus)

Alpha (α), used especially by Airbus, refers to the angle of attack (i.e. the angle of the wings to the airflow). If the angle is too steep and speed/power insufficient, the aircraft will Stall. To cope with wind shear and situations such as pilot inadvertence, where the aircraft might fatally lose lift near the ground, the auto-throttle system Airbuses have a protection mode (called alpha-floor) which automatically applies Takeoff/Go-Around power should the angle of attack exceed a certain limit (15 degrees in the case of Airbus 320).

ALPA: Airline Pilots Association

Pilots' Union. See IALPA.

Alphabet Letter (A, B, C...) Enunciation

Present-day globally used NATO version is as follows

Alfa, Bravo, Charley, Delta, Echo, Foxtrot,

Golf, Hotel, India, Juliet, Kilo, Lima,

Mike, November, Oscar, Papa, Quebec, Romeo,

Sierra, Tango, Uniform, Victor, Whisky, X-Ray,

Yankee, Zulu.

According to the FAA's AIM, numbers should be enunciated as

Wun, Too, Tree, Fow-er, Fife,
Six, Sev-en, Ait, Niner & Zero.

Apparently, *nine* enunciated by U.S. speakers can be confused with *five*, hence the use of *Niner.*

The use of whole word call sign prefixes such *United* for UA and *Speedbird* for British Airways, and suffixes such as *Heavy* to denote a jumbo-sized aircraft, makes exchanges with air traffic control longer but more easily understood since the listener has time to lock in mentally.

Altimeter

The key instrument indicating the height of the aircraft

- Barometric Altimeter

  Traditional altimeter using measurement of air pressure to determine height and the one mainly used because aircraft at the same place and height (and same reference pressure setting) will have the same reading, making it ideal for air traffic control separation of aircraft at different heights. Has small inset dial for inputting the reference pressure in millibars. Reference pressure to give height above the airport is called

QFE, and that for the height above mean seal level is called QNE. Reference pressures for an airport or area are given by ATC or automatic recorded broadcasts. In the U.S., a standard setting is entered when above 18,000ft, as there is little chance of hitting the ground and the only need is for all aircraft to have the same setting.

- Radio or Radar Altimeter

    Uses radio waves bounced off the ground to give the height. Gives true height above ground level (agl) at that moment. Radio altimeters can fluctuate wildly; say when the aircraft is near the ground and passing over a clump of trees. The synthesized vocal alerts (also see GPWS) regarding height above ground are based on radio altimeter data.

Altitude

Height of aircraft above sea level (QFE) shown by barometric altimeter adjusted for local barometric pressure, or with standard adjustment when above 18,000 ft (in U.S.). See QFE and QNE.

Aluminum (U.S.) Aluminium (U.K.)

Aluminum alloys are to varying degrees being replaced by composites and titanium in the latest airliners.

Aluminum shower [slang]

A mid-air collision.

Amelia Earhart, 1897-1937

The world-famous American aviatrix born in Kansas, who disappeared on a round-the-world exploit. Described as America's favorite missing person. See *Air Crashes and Miracle Landings*.

AMU: Audio Management Unit

Angle of Attack (AoA) (α)

Angle of the wings to the airflow.

Anhedral

Civilian aircraft usually have wings that are Dihedral (i.e. slope upwards as they project outwards from the fuselage). This gives them natural stability as the aircraft automatically rights itself after banking.

On the other hand, the wings of military aircraft such as fighters are often anhedral (i.e. slope downwards as they project outwards from the fuselage) to make them inherently unstable and hence more maneuverable. Computerized controls and stabilizers provide apparent stability.

Anti-Missile Technology

Shoulder-launched SAMS (Surface to Air Missiles) can be bought on the black market for less than $10,000, and are said to be in the hands of some 30 terrorist organizations. Civilian aircraft on an approach to an airport are particularly vulnerable as are long-haul flights taking off heavily laden with fuel and unable to climb away rapidly.

APU: Auxiliary Power Unit

Small power generating turbine usually situated at extreme rear end of aircraft. Used for generating electricity for onboard equipment and air-conditioning when aircraft on the ground and not connected to airport electricity supply. Also used to supply bleed air to start main engines.

With the increasing cost of fuel, greater use is being made of electricity supplied by the airport.

Approach

Final phase of a flight, requiring intense concentration, as the aircraft comes in to land.

Approach Control

Air traffic control unit responsible for handling aircraft as they Approach the airport for landing (after they have been Handed Off to them by the Center responsible for traffic in their region). In turn hands them off to the Tower for the actual landing. See Air Traffic Control (ATC).

Apron

Paved area at airport used for parking aircraft.

Artificial Horizon (AH)

Instrument showing the *Attitude* of the aircraft in the longitudinal axis (pitching up and down) and lateral axis (banking to left and right).

ASK: Available Seat Kilometers

Number of seats available multiplied by number of kilometers flown (usually by the whole fleet). Seats may not be available for a number of reasons, including the need to have one or more seats for members of the crew to rest. The larger long-haul aircraft have dedicated crew rest areas.

Ask The Pilot (book)

Ask The Pilot answers many of the questions passengers ask, and may well appeal to readers of the present dictionary.

The author, professional pilot Patrick Smith, selected the material from his excellent aviation blog on the website salon.com, where he comments on the latest aviation happenings, whether they be major accidents or minor gripes, such as annoying features of U.S. airport security checks.

ASRS: Aviation Safety Reporting System

Reporting system run by NASA of the U.S. for the confidential reporting of incidents. Similar to CHIRP or EUCARE.

Asymmetric Flight

Case where total thrust from engines on one side not equal to total thrust on the other, say when an engine has failed. Some four-engine aircraft are allowed to take off (without passengers) with just three engines to go for repairs. Usually only specially trained pilots are allowed to do this.

Recently, a British Airways aircraft with passengers on board, suffered an engine failure shortly after take-off from Los Angeles, with the pilots trying to fly on to London on three engines.

An unfavorable wind coupled with having to fly lower than usual with only three engines meant it could not reach London with the necessary fuel reserves, and had to land short at Manchester (U.K.).

Though passengers were not in any real danger as the aircraft had already taken off safely on four engines, the FAA argued with the airline and the U.K. authorities about imposing a maximum $25,000 fine. This raised the complicated question of jurisdiction in the case of international flights, for the British were arguing that, under their rules, continuing all the way on three engines was permissible. Indeed, four engine BA aircraft do sometimes come back for servicing to London on three engines. The author experiences such a situation in Japan, where the BA 747 he was about to board flew back to London on three engines, without passengers.

Asymmetric Warfare

Warfare with a great disparity in terms of size, weaponry and logistical support, usually meaning that the weaker side has to avoid squaring off and instead exploit the stronger side's weaknesses—with unsettling pin-prick attacks in vulnerable spots, better tactics, and subterfuge, perhaps causing him to over-react and alienate civilian populations or even tire of the whole enterprise.

Although the U.S. has a military unit called AWG (Asymmetric Warfare Group) set up in the context of the War on Terror advising on such warfare, some in the U.S. try to exclude operations against *terrorists* from this definition, since their inclusion would appear to ennoble them.

ATA: Air Transport Association of America

Trade association representing and promoting the interests of the major U.S. airlines.

ATC: Air Traffic Control

In the narrow sense, it is the controllers telling pilots by radio what to do, what not to do, and giving permissions to takeoff, land and so on. See Air Traffic Control.

ATC Clearance

Permission from ATC to operate according to set conditions.

For example, before taking off, an aircraft must obtain an ATC Clearance indicating what they are to do after takeoff, say

Climb to such and such a height, and proceed to....

ATI: Air Transport Intelligence [http://www.rati.com/]

To quote the website: ATI is the leading information source for the global air transport industry, providing you with essential real-time news and market data 24 hours a day.

It is part of the Reed Business Information Group, which includes *Flight International* and *flightglobal.com.*

ATIS Automated Terminal Information Service

Continuous (recorded) broadcast giving meteorological and other conditions at an airport.

ATPL: Airline Transport Pilot License

The highest qualification for a commercial pilot. See CPL.

ATSB: Australian Transport Safety Bureau

Australia's highly respected accident investigation authority.

In *Abstracts of References and Incidents*, Professor Peter Ladkin remarks that the ATSB reports are very-high quality documents and goes on to mention the ATSB's use of Professor Reason's work on the active and latent causes of accidents.

Attitude

The angle of the aircraft relative about the longitudinal and lateral axes relative to the horizon. Concerns pitch and roll.

Very important, since the behavior of an aircraft depends on its attitude, and of course speed and Flap settings.

Autoland

System permitting aircraft to land in poor or even zero visibility initially developed and introduced in the U.K. in the 1960s with the Trident airliner, although the Aerospatiale Caravelle was said to be the first airliner so equipped.

Autoland was not appreciated at first in the United States because zero visibility in the U.S. was normally associated with blizzards and blustery conditions precluding such landings anyway. Paradoxically, the pea soup fogs, which once made the British number one in the Autoland, field have largely disappeared due to clean air laws and the fact that coal is nowadays rarely being used to heat homes.

Autoland has now been perfected and fitted to many airliners where likely to be required, and found to work well, but has the great drawback that the presence of other aircraft can affect the ILS signals on which it depends.

This means aircraft have to be spaced out (kept twice as far or even further apart than normal when landing), which in turn means that airports already operating near their limits have to reduce traffic considerably, and hundreds of flights have to be delayed or cancelled. This was the case recently at London's Heathrow, where three days of foggy weather led to departing passengers having to wait in tents outside the airport buildings already crammed with people, or return home.

Automated External Defibrillator (AED)

New equipment carried on board airliners for dealing with passengers having heart attacks and heart stoppages.

Autopilot: A/P

Originally, the autopilot simply eliminated the need for pilots to hold an aircraft on course manually. They could tell it to fly a certain heading, at a certain height and at a speed controlled by the Auto-Throttle (A/T), which was particularly helpful in busy situations such as on taking off and climbing out where constant adjustments would otherwise have to be made to the throttle settings.

Subsequently, the instructions themselves took on a life of their own by being held or programmed in a system called Flight Director (F/D), which besides telling the autopilot what to do when switched on, could be shown on other instruments (Primary Display) with the pilots following it as if they were the autopilot. The Flight Director could also be programmed to take instructions from ground aids such as ILS landing systems and radio beacons.

Thus, the term autopilot really came to mean the *Autopilot/Flight Director system.*

Finally, to cap it all, we now have the FMS (Flight Management System) which like the computer "HAL" in the movie (film) *2001: A Space Odyssey* knows everything and is <u>able</u> to control much of the flight, telling the Autopilot-Flight Director and the pilots what to do.

Autorotation (Autogiro/Helicopter)

The movement alone of a rotor-supported craft through the air will make the rotor rotate and provide lift, and in fact, the autogiro with no engine driving the rotor works on this principal. Though helicopters do have engine-driven rotors, the rotors can rotate independently of the engine and, given sufficient forwards airspeed, keep rotating to allow the craft to come down safely—i.e. not drop like a stone if the engine fails.

AUW: All Up Weight

Total loaded weight of aircraft including usable fuel, passengers and freight, not only at take off, but also at any time during the flight.

BOW (Basic Operating Weight) is the weight of the empty aircraft itself, plus crew, drinking water, engine oil, hydraulic fluid, unusable fuel and anything else required at departure, while EW (Empty Weight) is BOW minus Crew.

Avgas: Aviation gasoline.

High-octane gasoline used for piston engines and UAVs. Lead—now largely banned for use in motor vehicles—is used to achieve the high octane number.

Also, differs from *mogas* (motor gasoline) in that it is made less volatile to prevent air locks at low atmospheric pressures.

Aviatrix

Female aviator—term used in early days of flying when female pilots were a relative rarity.

See http://www.aviationexplorer.com/

B- (B-17, B-29, B-52 ...)

The B stands for *bomber* and not for Boeing.

See Designations (U.S. military).

Babyflot

Term coined for the numerous small airlines spawned in the Russian Federation in recent years.

Unlike the more safety conscious Aeroflot from which the term is derived, they are said to be run by bean counters exerting great pressure (in the form of financial penalties on pilots) to save fuel, encouraging them to land the first time and even to fly above storms. In one case, an aircraft flew above its maximum height and in so doing became uncontrollable and crashed. Said that lax oversight by authorities and freedom from the fear of compensation suits means Babyflot minds are not focused on safety.

BAE: British Aerospace Engineering

Surprisingly in that it is not American, the third largest defense contractor in the world in terms of revenue from defense, though as 93% of its revenue comes from defense related work it is not quite so big as that third place might suggest. Surprisingly too, it is difficult to find the words for which the acronym BAE stand in any of their publicity material. Perhaps they should have come up with a new name such as *Thales* chosen by their French counterpart. See Thales.

BAE has resulted from the grouping together of many famous British companies, which often had themselves resulted from amalgamations of well-known companies involved in defense work.

Though aerospace and notably fighters come to mind, the company is involved in a wide range of activities including shipbuilding and armored vehicles.

Key markets and operating bases are Australia, Saudi Arabia, South Africa, Sweden, the U.K., and increasingly the U.S. Recently the company exercised its right to sell back its stake in EADS held by virtue of its Airbus shares in order to concentrate on the opportunities in the U.S. market.

For the public in the U.K., BAE is best known for the mammoth *Al Yamamah* contracts with Saudi Arabia, and latterly with the accusations of corruption surrounding them. They are actually a whole series of deals made since the nineteen-sixties for aircraft and technical support. Part of the reason for BAE's continued predominance in Saudi Arabia was the exclusion of U.S. companies due to sensibilities in the U.S. Congress about the possible use of such aircraft against Israel.

Balance Indicator

See Coordinated Flight.

Base Leg

Aircraft often have to fly in a rectangular pattern before landing at an airport, and the base leg is the one before the last right-angle turn placing the aircraft (on its final leg) in alignment with the runway for landing.

See Traffic Pattern.

Bathtub Curve

The rate at which products fail tends to be high immediately on entering service (referred to as *infant mortality*). Then for a lengthy period it remains very low (period referred to *as useful life*), before sharply rising, but as not as steeply as the initial fall, with these classed as *wear-out* failures.

The curve showing failure rate against passage of time (years in the case of airliners) happens to be like that of the traditional bathtub shape viewed from the side. That is almost straight down at the foot of the bath, with the bottom almost horizontal, and the head of the bath at one's back curving gently upwards.

Shoppers of electrical goods and computers are often conned into taking out expensive insurance just for the period when failures are least likely to occur, namely in the second and third year—the first year infant mortality period being covered by statutory guarantees anyway.

See LINKS (Dictionary) on OpenHatchBooks.com for image.

Behavior Detection Officers

New breed of officer at U.S. airports *studying body language and facial cues of passengers for signs of bad intentions*. Usually work in pairs, with one performing an apparently mundane task—such as handing back belongings after X-ray examination, handing over the tray for metallic objects, handing back documents, helping with baggage, or openly questioning passenger about reason for their journey and their intentions—while his partner looks out for give-away signs.

Based on the highly successful Israeli El Al methods—but not usually so intrusive—and the work of Professor Ekman, et al. into the use of *micro-expressions* to identify hidden emotions. Attempts to develop software coupled with video cameras to perform the same task are being attempted but proving especially difficult as cues vary according to culture.

BFU: Bundestelle für Flugenfalluntersuchung

German Federal Bureau of Aircraft Accident Investigation

Bleed Air

Air bled off from main engines is used for cabin pressurization/cabin air renewal, and sometimes to start other engines. One disadvantage is that an engine fault, say rubbing of fan blades on rubber skirting, can lead to the introduction of smoke or fumes into the cabin. Bleed air from the APU (Auxiliary Power Unit) is often used to spin the fan blades of the main engines when starting them.

One novelty of the new Boeing 787 is that bleed air from the engines will not be used to pressurize the cabin.

Black Boxes (CVR & FDR)

Misnomer used by the media after a crash to describe the CVR (Cockpit Voice Recorder) and FDR (Flight Data Recorder) that should have information about what happened on the flight prior to the disaster.

Colored orange rather than black to be easily visible, they are designed to withstand crashes, fires and immersion down to 20,000ft in water. They also incorporate radio beacons to help their location for 30 days even under water. In addition, many modern aircraft have Quick Access Recorders (QAR) that record not only information similar to that recorded by the FDR, but also such parameters as brake temperatures, brake torque and tire pressures.

As their name implies, they provide information for immediate use by maintenance personnel and the company. They are neither designed to withstand major crashes or intense fire nor located to minimize damage in the event of a crash.

Boeing

> This entry for Boeing is much shorter than that for Airbus because Boeing's much longer history is covered by the entries for the various aircraft produced.
>
> Note that entries for Boeing's civilian aircraft are listed under the number alone without the Boeing suffix.

After taking over McDonnell Douglas, which once dashed the great Lockheed's hopes of making a commercial success of its wide-body TriStar (by entering the market sooner with its unlucky and in some ways technically inferior DC-10), Boeing now reigns supreme as regards airliner production in the U.S..

Perhaps living on its laurels, Boeing some years back went through a difficult patch, accused of constantly making the wrong policy decisions and being unadventurous, in contrast to the earlier days when it bet the company on the radically new 747, and on the 707 before that. In the ten years before what many consider to be the groundbreaking 787 the company had not come up with a really new aircraft. That said, with technology evolving faster than in the past, airframers are increasingly conscious of the danger of investing vast sums in developing what may prove to be a LastGen aircraft. Thus, Boeing may have been wise not to take the plunge too soon.

Anyway, Boeing is now apparently going from strength to strength despite its own production problems with its 787 and 747-8.

Boneyard

U.S. term for various sites, usually in dry isolated places, used to keep unwanted aircraft. Usually, these are older aircraft, but sometimes relatively new ones or even brand new ones straight from the manufacturer at times of a slump, such as after 9/11. The most well known aviation boneyard is the one in the Mojave Desert in southwestern U.S.A.

Brace Position

Passengers with seat belts attached in conventional forward-facing (as opposed to rearward-facing) seats would flip forward in a crash due to the deceleration. This would result in their hitting their head on the back of the seat in front, suffering a body whiplash, and possibly having their shins broken on the seat in front.

To try to preclude this, passengers are told to adopt a brace position that differs slightly from airline to airline. Some people believe that airlines tell passengers to adopt the brace position to ensure they will die, since insurance payouts for dead passengers are less than for those needing long-term medical treatment and care.

That is untrue. Adopting the brace position reduces injuries and perhaps more importantly increases ones chances of being in a fit condition to evacuate before being overcome by smoke—the major causes of fatalities in many cases. See Seat Belts.

Bugs

Used to be the sliding markers on the scales of mechanical instruments to show key points, just as one might have on a thermostat in one's home. Now with the 'glass cockpit' displays, the settings for height, airspeed, etc. in the Flight Director/Autopilot are marked by 'bugs' (markers) on the scales in the Primary Flight Display without the need for awkward physical manipulation.

Bulkhead, Rear

From the point of view of safety, the most important bulkhead on an airliner is the rear bulkhead, which is like a champagne cork preventing the pressurized air in the cabins from flowing out of the tail. However, unlike corks inserted in the small-diameter neck of the bottle, rear bulkheads in airliners are usually just behind the toilets where the diameter of the fuselage (taking into account the cargo space under the floor) is considerable.

To minimize weight these bulkheads are made of thin aluminum panels cut in odd shapes before being joined together to produce a dome that is concave when viewed from the cabin side from where the pressure is exerted.

There have been rare cases where these 'jigsaw puzzle structures' have failed in flight—including the worst-ever single-aircraft disaster where a Japan Airlines 747 meandered around for 30 minutes due to key parts of its tail being blown off by the gush of air caused by failure of the rear bulkhead.

Bumpy Landing (Hard Landing)

Under Touchdown in the entry on Landing, we mention cases where a hard landing is preferable. When in May 2010, an Air India Express Boeing 737-800 overshot the runway and its 90-meter long spillover area, plunged into a ravine, and burst into flames claiming 158 lives, one theory immediately advanced as to the cause was that the airline had told its pilots to ensure they made soft landings.

Bunt

Maneuver whereby the pilots push the nose down so suddenly that weightlessness (negative G) is produced.

A bunt followed by severe rolling can be used to try to throw hijackers off their feet.

C (Computer)

Readers should not allow themselves to be overwhelmed by the repeated appearance of the word computer and its abbreviation "C" in describing controls, equipment and software used in an aircraft. Whereas in the old days, many functions used to be purely mechanical, now almost anything involves IT (Information Technology) rather like the gas boiler for heating ones home. Many of the systems are subsystems. For instance, there is even an SEC (Spoiler/Elevator Computer) and SFEC (Slat/Flap Control Computer) and most of what they do is to regulate how the components work together.

Though linked, the computers are usually separate entities to facilitate maintenance (by replacing a module) and because specialist hardware can take the load off central processors rather like the graphics card in a PC taking much of the graphics burden off the shoulders of the main processor. In addition, failure of a component is not likely to lead to a generalized catastrophic failure.

Boeing's new 787 Dreamliner is attempting to go a step further by integrating all the systems in one computer, thus saving weight. However, achieving this without any risk of a failure is proving difficult, though other factors delaying the maiden flight by some 30 months gave the programmers more time than they expected.

CAM: Cockpit Area Microphone

Abbreviation used in transcriptions of cockpit voice recordings to indicate words said in cockpit. As there are several, these are sometimes referred to as CAM 1, CAM 2, etc. in accident reports.

Canard

Besides meaning a planted or false story, the French word *Canard* means Duck.

In aviation, it means having the horizontal stabilizers and elevators sticking out of the fuselage in front on the wings instead of having them at the tail. Seen on some business jets and on the Wright brothers' machines at the beginning of the Twentieth Century.

Capitol

The Capitol Building in Washington DC houses the Congress of the United States. As a high white dominating building at the end of the long grassy Mall, it would have made it an easy target for the fourth aircraft hijacked on Nine-Eleven, which supposedly it had been.

Captain

Nevertheless, nowadays with CRM (Crew Resource Management) captains are obliged to consider the views of their colleagues. (See Chirp)

The captain normally sits in left-hand seat, as traditionally many of the turns ordered by ATC for holding patterns and approaches were left turns and by sitting on the left the captain could check where aircraft was about to go by looking out of his side window.

CAT: Clear Air Turbulence

Category (visibility for IFR approach)
In order to make clear what is possible when landing under Instrument Flight Rules (IFR) in bad weather, runways are classified by the ICAO according to their nature and ILS equipment) and by the FAA as in the table on the next page.
The Decision Height is the height at which the pilot must decide whether to land or not, and the Minimum Runway Visibility Range (RVR) is the distance that can be seen down the runway—usually measured automatically by equipment alongside the runway.

Categories of ILS Approaches			
Category	Minimum Decision height	Minimum Runway Visibility Range	Remarks
I	200 feet	2400 feet	
I	200 feet	1800 feet	With touchdown zone and runway centerline lighting.
II	100 feet	1200 feet	Half the minimums of a standard Cat I approach
IIIa	100 feet	700 feet	
IIIb	50 feet	150 to 700 feet	
IIIc	No DH	No RVR limitation	[Completely blind landing—very rare]

Data from Aeronautical Information Manual, AIM, (FAA.gov).

Not only runways, but also pilots have to be classed according to what category landings they can perform. Sometimes cabin crews have alarmed passengers by telling them *the pilot cannot land the plane,* when all they meant was that he or she did not have the right qualifications for the visibility at the airport in question and that they must diverts.

Cayley, George

English baronet who studied birds and carried out experiments using an aerofoil attached to the end of a rotating spar to measure lift as it passed through the air, and thereby found flight was possible with forward motion through the air without flapping.

According to Phil Scott who wrote a book on the subject, Cayley made his coachman the first adult to fly in a heavier-than-air craft by putting him in a glider and rolling it downhill on a windy day in 1853—fifty years before the Wright brothers. He had worked out the principle years before but had put it on the back burner because of the impossibility of finding an engine at that time with the necessary power-to-weight ratio. Was he the true groundbreaker?

CDL: Configuration Deviation List

CDU: Control/Display Unit

Intimidating-looking cockpit instrument resembling an expensive old-fashioned calculator used for inputting and checking data in the so-called glass cockpit.

Ceiling

Has two meanings

- The height of the cloud base when the sky is overcast or clouds are virtually continuous.
- The maximum height at which an aircraft can operate.

Handling at extreme heights can be very tricky both as regards flying characteristics of aircraft and performance of engines. See Mach Number and Coffin Corner.

Center: Air Route Traffic Control Center

Center rather than full name (ATC Center) is used. (e.g. New York Center or Boston Center). Responsible for through traffic over a wide region and which normally follows airways. See Airways.

CFIT: Controlled Flight into Terrain

CFIT simply means the pilots fly the aircraft—under control—into terrain.

There are warning systems in the cockpit, which make a whooping sound and blare out *Terrain! Terrain! PULL UP! PULL UP!* if there, is a danger of this happening. However, they were not of much avail if the aircraft had a high mountain or cliff looming above it. Future warning systems using GPS and terrain databases should help solve that problem. See GPWS.

CFR: Current Flight Report

Chapter 11 (of U.S. Bankruptcy Code)

Form of bankruptcy in the U.S., which allows companies to continue operating protected from claims from creditors, and under which contracts such as labor union contracts are moot. The aim is to give the company time to reorganize and many emerge stronger from Chapter 11. With major U.S. airlines often operating under Chapter 11 and hence unshackled from commitments undertaken in historically more profitable times, non-U.S. carriers (unable to benefit from such legislation) claim they are disadvantaged.

Checklist

As mentioned in *Air Crashes and Miracle Landings,*
  In *Commercial Aviation Safety*, Alexander Wells says

> It is ironic that with all of the sophisticated and costly devices on board an aircraft and those supporting the aircraft through the air traffic control system (ATC), the most important guardian of the safety of the plane and its occupants is a single piece of paper, the checklist.

> It is the linchpin of aviation operations, not only for pilots in the cockpit, but also for those who are making and maintaining the aircraft.

The use of checklists in aviation is said to have originated with the Boeing B-17 Flying Fortress where the pilots demonstrating the first model failed to release the control lock to prevent the aircraft blowing away in the wind when parked.

Chimes

Audible chimes in the cockpit to draw attention to certain events or abnormal situations, which are not necessarily serious but require that the pilots pay attention to a certain instrument.

Audible chimes in the passenger cabin are signals from the pilots to the cabin crew who could be anywhere and are thus audible to the passengers as well.

Chimes heard in the cabin are also referred to as *dings*, with them having different meanings according to the number. For instance, the pilots can ding the cabin crew to indicate they want to talk over the intercom for transmission of more complex information. A frequently heard ding after takeoff tells the cabin crew the aircraft has reached sufficient height for communication with the pilots. See Sterile Cockpit Rule.

On some airlines, the greater the number of dings, the worse the situation.

China

Rapid expansion of civil aviation in China is leading to an increasing demand for pilots. More than 90% trained at Civil Aviation Flight University of China (CAFUC).

According to Jane's Transport News Briefs - 8 June 2007 – China Southern Airlines is going to allow some pilots to pay for their own training at the airline's training facilities in Western Australia, which has the advantage of much empty airspace.

On the manufacturing side, China will be before long a force with which to be reckoned. Some say that while Boeing is jousting in the WTO and in political circles over alleged unfair subsidies given to Airbus, other countries such as China and Brazil supporting their aircraft industries to an even greater extent are forging ahead.

China Airlines

Airline based in Taiwan. Not to be confused with the mainland's Air China.

Suffered a series of disastrous accidents, attributed by some to the double-punch of

- The deference to elders once the norm in Asian societies
- The fact that many pilots came from the military, where the querying of a senior's orders was out of the question. See CRM.

CHIRP: Confidential Human Factors Incident Reporting

A confidential reporting system in the U.K. by which professional pilots and ATC staff report incidents arising from human errors for analysis by the RAF Institute of Aviation Medicine at Farnborough.

Initially was set up to deal with the problem of overbearing but fallible captains—nowadays becoming extinct with the stress on CRM.

See EUCARE and ASRS.

CFDS: Centralized Fault Display System

Clean Configuration

Term frequently mentioned in the context of the dangerous wake turbulence produced by large heavy airliners climbing out from airport under high power in *clean configuration* (with flaps, slats or undercarriage retracted = nothing sticking out).

Cleanskin

A term originally used by the security services to describe an operative (their own or their opponent's) with no compromising history, connections, or antecedents, that might enable the target to detect him or her.

Security services and police forces are increasingly applying the term to *homegrown terrorists* who fit that description and carry out shootings and the detonation of bombs in their home country. The near impossibility of identifying such individuals makes it very difficult to preempt such attacks.

Clear Air Turbulence (CAT)

Present-day weather radar cannot detect turbulence in clear air, as there are no large particles such as raindrops to detect. Cases occur from time to time, where the aircraft may suddenly drop without warning causing unbelted passengers and food trolleys to hit the cabin ceiling, only to fall back dangerously.

In the future, so-called laser radar (Lidar) using a laser beam shone ahead of the aircraft may help detect it. Currently, the most valuable forewarnings are from aircraft ahead.

Clearway

A hoped for area free of unforgiving obstacles before and beyond a runway. In the interest of safety, there are recommended distances, but with conurbations encroaching on airports or vice-versa, it is not always possible to comply.

With the decrease in other types of accidents, runway overruns, especially on landing in bad weather, are coming high on the list of as regards frequency of incidents and accidents. Where there is insufficient space, a specially devised arresting zone could often improve safely significantly at some cost. See EMAS.

CMC: Central Maintenance Computer

CMS: Central Maintenance System

Cockpit

In a recent letter to the U.K.'s *Flight International*, reader Anthony Jones said one of his pet hates was the use of the term cockpit—especially by Americans—for what should be called the flight deck. For him, the cockpit was a pit or hole in fuselages used long ago to house the engine cocks or controls. However, others suggest it has nautical origins.

Nevertheless, the term cockpit is gaining increasing currency in the phrase Glass Cockpit.

Cockpit Voice Recorder (CVR)

System recording

- Pilots conversations between themselves
- Radio communications with air traffic control etc.
- Extraneous sounds captured by cockpit mikes (CMs) placed at various points on the flight deck.

The sound data is stored in a so-called Black Box, usually situated in the tail and designed to withstand crashes and any subsequent fire.

Extraneous sounds and particularly the pitch of the engines recorded by the cockpit mikes (CMs) can be used in accident enquiries to determine their rate of rotation.

Surprising as it may seem today, pilots' unions once tenaciously resisted introduction of CVRs on the grounds of invasion of privacy, just as they are now doing with regard to Cockpit **Video** Recorders.

Despite being mandatory in the U.S., British pilots' union opposition meant they were not mandatory in the U.K. until a British European Airways (BEA) Trident crashed shortly after takeoff from London's Heathrow in 1972 with all on board except the captain killed by the shock of the belly flop. A post mortem showed the captain was already dead due to a heart attack.

Someone had moved the droop (slat) control lever just at the time the aircraft was flying slowly on its climb out to comply with noise abatement regulations. This resulted in a Change of Configuration Stall.

Investigators were unable to determine whether it had been the captain, his rookie copilot, or even someone else, who pulled back that droops (Slats) lever. The British Government as a result faced down the union and adopted the U.S. policy with regard to CVRs, making them mandatory shortly afterwards.

The ill-fated Egypt Air flight ex-JFK in 1999, where investigators were unable to prove irrefutably that the aircraft was purposely crashed by a pilot, was similar in that respect, but failed to bring about the installation of Cockpit VIDEO Recorders—something that is on the NTSB's Most Wanted list.

Cockpit Video Recorder

On the NTSB's MOST WANTED LIST as one of the ten most sought-after measures for improving air safety. However, as was the case for the cockpit voice recorder above, the pilots' unions are very much opposed, with the U.S. pilots' union calling *it fool's gold* in that in their opinion it would not improve safety. In addition, they say that the assurances regarding privacy and data protection they received before the introduction of CVRs have proved worthless.

It is ironic, that they higher up the food chain one goes, the greater the opposition to video surveillance (to which members of the ordinary public are subjected daily). Logically those with the greatest responsibility, such as prime ministers and presidents, able to destroy the world with nuclear weapons should be monitored most of all! In fact, they are monitored the least, so pilots are in good company.

Cameras watching the controls and instrument panels would show what the pilots see and do, and in many cases absolve them from accusations.

Cockpit-Centric (as opposed to *Tower-Centric*)

The future NextGen (ATC) system envisages a more cockpit-centric approach, with pilots less dependent on the Tower for information and instructions.

Although NextGen is going to require considerable investment, the philosophy applies at the simplest level as well. For example *Air Transport World* reported the award to Sensis of a contract for *Runway Status Lights* at the busiest airports which would automatically come on should it be dangerous to cross or enter a runway without the controller being in the loop. There would also be *takeoff hold* lights working on a similar principle.

Coffin Corner

This refers to the relatively little latitude pilots have as regards airspeed when cruising at great heights. If they go too close to Mach 1 (the speed of sound), the aircraft can misbehave and stall; if they go too slowly they risk stalling in the thin air.

Sophisticated computerized controls mean the aircraft can usually maintain the correct speed automatically, making it seem a routine boring situation. However, if the controls fail to do so, say because the probes (pitot tubes) are blocked by ice and giving false data regarding airspeed, the pilots do not have much leeway, and a disaster can easily happen—hence the term *coffin corner.* Term widely mentioned in connection with the loss of the Air France A-330 en route from Rio de Janeiro to Paris in 2009.

Comet (de Havilland Comet)

Britain's de Havilland Comet, the world's first jetliner (first revenue passengers May 1952), stole a march on the Americans, and with its elegant design looked as though it would be a tremendous success, despite its limited number of passengers (initially 44 in great comfort) and rather limited range, which it made up for with its much greater speed.

Some initial crashes and overruns on takeoff were dismissed as being due to over-confident pilots not appreciating the handling characteristics and Rotating too early when taking off in hot conditions. It was later found that that the problem was more complicated than it first appeared, and that there was a known design fault with regard to airflow over the leading edge of the wing and inability of the engines to gulp-in air, both being evident at high angles of attack.

However, these were the least of its problems, as there followed a couple of mysterious disasters where aircraft well into their flights suffered catastrophic failures and broke up in mid-air.

Winston Churchill the then prime minister ordered that everything be done to find the cause. Engineers subjected an entire Comet airframe to pressurized water tests to simulate the cycles to which the Comet airframe was subjected in operation. Finally, these tests revealed a failure point due to fatigue and in addition, that stress concentrations around the square windows were much greater than expected.

The Comet 1 never saw service again, while the Comet 2 (with small round windows as opposed to the previous square ones was used without incident by Britain's Royal Air Force who operated it for years but with lower pressurization.

The rather larger Comet 4 later entered service over the Atlantic, but was superseded by the arrival only 3 weeks later of the Boeing 707, which was much larger and more efficient to operate. Had de Havilland not been first, other manufacturers could well have suffered the same fate.

Composites

New materials such as carbon fiber are replacing parts traditionally made of metal such as aluminum alloy to give a better strength to weight ratio. Usually, they consist of a combination of materials to try to combine the qualities of them all. Sometimes aluminum alloy netting or foil is included to avoid the creep associated with plastics.

In the 787 Dreamliner, metal netting has been incorporated in certain parts to prevent damage from lightning—though not likely to cause a crash, repairing the damage caused could be expensive. Greatest worry has been that checking for cracks and so on is much more difficult than for electro-conductive metals. See SHM (Structural Health Monitoring).

Compressor Stall

Situation produced by the abnormal flow of air through turbine or jet engine caused by a number of factors including ingestion of birds and Side Slipping. Sometimes results in loud bangs.

Often no damage to engine, but sometimes engine will flame out, be irretrievably damaged, or catch fire. Some stalls affecting entire engine referred to as compressor surges. Though somewhat frightening for passengers, usually not serious.

Concorde (Supersonic Airliner)

Beautiful supersonic airliner developed at tremendous cost to U.K. and French taxpayers. Only 12 were made, and virtually given away to those two countries' flag carriers.

The aircraft failed to sell internationally because

- Its limited range meant that it was only viable on relatively short routes such as between London and New York, with Paris to New York being near the limit. Could not be used for the long transpacific routes where the time saved would have been considerable.

- Noise problems and the sonic boom meant that countries would not let their airports be used for stopovers.

- Perhaps partly because of sour grapes, use in the U.S. was very restricted.
- Fuel consumption was too high.

British Airways and Air France operated it for prestige, with BA finding it quite profitable.

However, when it crashed in flames after taking off for New York from Paris' Charles de Gaulle airport, it statistically, went from one of the safest airliners to one of the most dangerous after the supersonic 5-star airliner crashed in flames into a 2-star hotel just outside Paris' Charles de Gaulle airport in 2000.

Configuration

The state of the aircraft as regards deployment of flaps, slats, undercarriage, and so on.

A *change of configuration* stall is a stall that occurs without a change in airspeed simply because the flap or slat settings are (inadvertently) changed. See *Clean Configuration.*

Commonality

Commonality is the concept whereby the manufacturer uses not only the same parts, but also whole sections of the airframe over a whole range of different aircraft. This cost-cutting approach is particularly favored by Boeing.

Computer Assisted Design: CAD

Aircraft manufacturers depend on computers for much of their design work.

Less well known is the role computers play in predicting the behavior of the materials making up the aircraft and engines, saving considerable expense carrying out physical trials, and theoretically improving safety. They have vast databases showing how metals in particular behave—something not available to the makers of the de Havilland Comet, the world's first jetliners which crashed due to metal fatigue.

These programs work well except when over-extrapolated, as in the case of the Challenger Space Shuttle Disaster, where foam cladding breaking off from the fuel tank during launch fatally damaged the protective tiles making up the heat shield. On re-entry at high speed into the Earth's atmosphere, the hot gases generated by the friction penetrated the hull where it had been bared due to impact from the foam. Disaster followed.

The Boeing computer program created and calibrated to predict the effect of tiny particles on the tiles had been over-extrapolated (not by Boeing) to predict the effect of large chunks.

Connectors (airlines based on strategic hubs)

Certain well-managed airlines operating out of geographically well-placed hubs and able to provide quality service have been very successful. A notable example is Singapore Airlines. In that case, the fact that other countries wanted to use the hub made it easier to obtain landing rights in the days when that was more difficult than now.

Dubai in the Middle East used to be a stopover/refueling point merely known to most passengers for offering duty-free goods in the middle of the night. However, now in what the *Economist* on June 3, 1910 dramatically headlined as *Super-Duper-Connectors from the Gulf*, three airlines, Dubai's Emirates, Qatar Airways from Qatar and Etihad from Abu Dhabi are establishing themselves as major players based on hubs such as Dubai, even threatening the predominance of erstwhile flag carriers such as British Airways and Air France-KLM.

The *Economist* goes on to say that the new generation of aircraft can reach almost any major city on earth from there, while rather nearer there are of billions of people in Asia and Africa previously neglected by the airline industry. These airlines have the advantages of Singapore Airlines as regards good management and not many union problems. They may also benefit, perhaps to a lesser degree than Singapore Airlines, from the fact that working as cabin crew has some prestige.

Though accused by established carriers in the US and Europe of benefitting unfairly as regards the cost of fuel and landing fees, this is not so. Where they do benefit, is from being able to take risks and being able to find the necessary funds. This is particularly true of Emirates who have gone out on a limb by placing a firm order for 32 Airbus 380 superjumbos in addition to the 58 already on order. This is four or five times more than airlines such as Qantas (20), Singapore Airlines (19), Lufthansa (15), Air France –KLM (12) and British Airways (12). Such as large order is likely to mean they have obtained very good terms from which they could benefit cost wise for many years to come, ironically like the low-cost carriers easyJet and Ryanair who were able to purchase new aircraft cheaply.

Constellation/Lockheed Constellation [military 1943] [civil 1945] 850+*

* The total produced is for both versions, with many of the military versions converted to civil use after the Second World War.

A beautiful four-engine airliner with a distinctive triple tail conceived just before World War II, with much input from Howard Hughes.

According to Wikipedia, it partly owes its elegant appearance to the fact that its fuselage has a continuously variable profile with no two bulkheads the same shape. The article further points out that this mode of construction is very expensive and was replaced by the mostly tube-shape of modern airliners—the tube being more resistant to pressurization changes and cheaper to build. The legendry Howard Hughes apparently greatly influenced the design.

In the 1950s, it became a frequent sight at major airports all round the world as the first serious long-distance pressurized airliner. Although the arrival of the ill-fated British de Havilland Comet had presaged the end of the Constellation's reign over long-distance routes, it was the entry into commercial service of the Boeing 707 in 1978, and subsequently the DC-8 that quickly rendered the Constellation obsolete for such routes.

While the Constellation depended on its powerful Wright R3350 engines for its success, these were something of a liability. Indeed, the FAA ordered that the aircraft be taken out of civilian service until modified after incidents in the early months.

Cruising speed was 340 mph (295 kt, 547 km/h) at 22,600 ft (6,890 m). Could carry more than 100 passengers but would usually carry rather fewer in configurations that were more comfortable.

Contaminated Runway

Term used to describe a runway where something on the surface prevents the tires getting a grip. That something can often be ice, but a deep layer of water can be equally pernicious as at high speeds the aircraft tires will aquaplane, making the brakes virtually useless. See the 100-M.P.H. Qantas overrun at Bangkok described in *Air Crashes and Miracle Landings*.

Contrails/Vapor Trails

Vapor trails formed way behind the aircraft due to the added water produced from the burning of the fuel pushing the humidity of the air over 100%, so that water droplets and ice-crystals are formed.

These differ from the vapor trails seen coming off the flaps and wingtips when aircraft are landing or taking off in extremely humid conditions. These are simply the result of condensation brought about by the cooling brought about by the drop in pressure as air compressed under the flaps comes out from under them, and from pressure drops occurring in the wingtip vortices.

Control Area/Zone

Control Area is airspace where all aircraft are subject to ATC control. Control Zone is similar except that it applies specifically to a designated zone encompassing an airfield and its environs.

Controlled Airspace

The ICAO defines classes of airspace from A to G, with A being the most restrictive as regards flight rules, and with F and G being essentially unrestricted airspace. There have been moves to reduce the number to three, namely those roughly equivalent to the current C, E and G. In fact, a

Cc

number of countries including the U.S. work with a reduced number. Finally, there is Special Use Airspace (SUA) where the letter-based classifications may still apply but where only certain aircraft, say military aircraft, are allowed to operate.

Convair 880/890   [1960] 65/ [1961] 37

The Convair 880 was a jet airliner designed by the Convair Division of General Dynamics to compete with the somewhat larger Boeing 707 and Douglas DC-8. General Dynamics terminated the project after building only 65, losing an enormous sum of money, and demonstrating how risky manufacturing airliners can be. The company also produced a stretched version, the Convair 990, that also failed to sell as hoped with only 37 built, thus compounding the loss made on the 880.

The Convair 990 was notable for being able to fly slightly faster than competing jets, but lost out because of fuel consumption, range and passenger capacity.

Coordinated Flight

Simply means flying the aircraft with appropriate banking so that it feels as if it is level when turning—somewhat like a car going round a corner with the road cambered perfectly for the given speed. This is achieved mainly by correct coordination of rudder and aileron movements, but also partly by applying some elevator to stop the aircraft pitching down and sinking due to the banking.

A *Balance Indicator* operating somewhat like a spirit level enables the pilots to achieve this. Autopilots can perform this perfectly, and pilots will generally use them to make changes of course automatically with the passengers not noticing anything unless looking out of the window.

Coordinates

Geographical position on Earth's surface (or above that point on surface) usually expressed in terms of Latitude (degrees and minutes of arc north or south of Equator) and Longitude (degrees and minutes of arc west or east of Greenwich (U.K.)). Note: 1 Nautical Mile = 1 minute of arc. (Therefore circumference of the Earth = 360 x 60 = 21,000 nm).

Though the entering of coordinates into navigation systems enables pilots to reach their desired destination or waypoint almost effortlessly, there is the danger, just as with motorists' SATNAVs, that erroneous coordinates may be entered with disastrous results. Thus, airlines insist pilots cross-check when entering coordinates and use other means en route to confirm they are they are actually where they should be.

Corrosion

With some airliners being 20 or 30 years old, corrosion or rather checking for corrosion can be costly. There is also the phenomenon called

52

stress-assisted corrosion whereby the flexing of the material produces microscopic cracks on the surface, which increase the rate of corrosion.

In the case of metals, electrical testing methods can be used to detect potential points of failure. However, these methods do not work with composites unless conductive material is especially incorporated.

Cost Benefit (Your Life = $2,700,000?)

In the context of the regulatory framework, such as in the FAA in the U.S., cost-benefit comes to the fore in deciding whether a new safety feature should be made mandatory. Various formulae are used to calculate the value of a life, not only in terms of lost earnings, but also terms of the loss to society and family. One figure quoted for the U.S. some years ago **was** U.S. $2.7 million. Other countries would set the value of a life lower in monetary terms, but the U.S. is the arbiter at the moment.

The phrase *Tombstone Mentality* is not officially used, but sums up the recognized fact that safety improvements are very often only introduced after a serious accident causing legislators, the media, and the public to focus on the problem and demand immediate action.

Counter-intuitivity

Humans evolved, at least in recent times, as creatures walking, running, jumping, or sitting on terra firma, and as described under the entry *Spatial Disorientation* find their intuitive reactions are liable to be inappropriate when in the air.

Other situations where intuitivity can make matters worse are

- When all controls have failed and the pilots are trying to control the aircraft by engine power alone, they intuitively tend to apply power just at the wrong moment only to make the Dutch Roll even worse. See *Intelligent Flight Control System (IFCS)* where NASA is trying to see whether neural network (NN) software can solve such problems;
- The case where the Americans Airlines pilot is said to have attributed the extreme yawing of his A300 entirely to the wake turbulence from another aircraft when in fact his extreme one-side-to-the-other rudder movements were no doubt exacerbating it, and ended up with him breaking off the tailfin.

Country of Registration

See Aircraft Registration Codes.

CPDLC: Controller-Pilot Data Link Communications

CPL: Commercial Pilot License

Basic license required to pilot an aircraft for hire as opposed to a PPL (Private Pilots License). Issued for the different categories of aircraft, and importantly with various ratings specifying what the pilot is allowed to do.

Passengers have sometimes been alarmed to hear flight attendants say a pilot cannot land the aircraft at such and such a place when all they mean is that he or she is not certified for landing in such weather conditions. Note that in the U.S., the term *certificate* rather than *license* is used. With the exception of military pilots, pilots generally obtain a PPL first.

Crab (landing *crabwise*)

When landing with a significant crosswind, the pilot points the nose a little into the wind so as not to be blown to one side in a move called crabbing. In effect, the aircraft is flying in a straight line down the runway, but with the airframe and wheels at an angle to it. At the last moment, the pilot will straighten up so as not to damage the undercarriage when the wheels touch the runway. The pilot may also dip the wing into the wind to produce a sideslip, which is another way of compensating for the crosswind. The pilot would then level the wings at the last moment before touchdown. In most cases, it is a combination of these two maneuvers.

These require skill and practice, as dramatically demonstrated by the scary 2008 video showing a Lufthansa A320 landing in a crosswind. By crabbing and dipping her wing into the wind, the pilot seems to be successfully bringing the aircraft down on the runway centerline, but just as the wheels are about to touch (at which point the spoilers would automatically come up forcing the aircraft onto the ground), a gust blows the windward wing upwards, and the aircraft sideways. The windward wing is raised so high that the tip of the other wing scrapes the ground with neither pilot realizing it. The pilot aborts the landing and lands safely on a runway more suitably angled to the prevailing wind.

Landing Gear is very robust and can withstand a certain amount of misalignment with the runway and in consequence, few aircraft require landing gear that can swivel to accommodate any misalignment. An exception is the B-52 bomber, which cannot dip a wing into the wind on landing due to the proximity to the ground of the outboard engines and fuel tanks slung under the Anhedral wings.

Criminalization (Antithesis of "No-Blame")

Most aviation accidents can be attributed to a whole host of factors as demonstrated by Professor Reason (sic), and even an error at the frontline by a pilot can be often attributed to failures in training and selection. The accepted view in the industry was that causes—and in particular potential causes—should be sought rather than blame attributed, as this was the only way that pilots (and mechanics) would come forward and the truth be revealed.

Recently there has been a tendency for judiciaries to seek criminal prosecutions, which many in the aviation community think could be counterproductive.

CRM: CREW RESOURCE MANAGEMENT

The Mantra for safe airline operations.

CRM is a formalized approach to getting crewmembers to work as a team with consultation, yet clear allocation of tasks. Introduced by United Airlines using techniques from business management following an incident at Portland in 1978 in which the crew were so concerned about a possible problem with the undercarriage that they failed to consider fuel-depletion. Originally stood for *Cockpit* Resource Management, but subsequently changed to *Crew* Resource Management to imply it included all concerned—flight attendants, mechanics, and so on. CRM is applicable in many other domains—especially medicine.

Crosswind

In the old days, many airfields would have three runways in a triangular configuration so that one of them would very likely permit a landing or take off directly into the wind or not far from it.

Nowadays large airports with a tremendous amount of traffic will very likely have two parallel runways orientated to cope with the most prevailing wind and allow take offs and landing to take place simultaneously.

This means that on some days the crosswind component may be considerable. Airlines have limits on the maximum crosswind component acceptable. Though an aircraft may be able to *takeoff* in a very strong crosswind, the airline has to bear in mind that the aircraft might have to return and land there in the event of a mechanical problem manifesting itself after V_1.

CRT: Cathode Ray Tube [Monitor/Screen/Display]

There is no good term to describe the various types of display now possible. As might be expected, CRT appears in accounts of incidents occurring in the older days.

Cycle (usually equal to number of flights)

Aircraft cabins are pressurized so that passengers can stay alive and relatively comfortable whatever the height. This difference in pressure between the inside and outside, means the fuselage expands due to the *increasing* difference in air pressure between the inside and outside as the aircraft goes up and contracts due to the *decreasing* difference as it comes down. This expansion and contraction that associated with any flight reaching a significant height is referred to as a *cycle*.

The number of cycles to which an aircraft has been subjected is significant as metals such as aluminum alloy are liable to crack if bent repeatedly beyond their elastic limit one way and then the other. [Anyone can see this for themselves by taking a thick copper wire and bending it back and forth. At some point, it will suddenly become brittle and snap.]

Ever since the ill-fated Comet 1 airliner, manufacturers have taken particular care in their designs to ensure stress is distributed and not concentrated at particular points where the elastic limit might be exceeded. Nevertheless, the number of cycles rather than age in years is a better indicator of the likely condition of an aircraft.

CVR: Cockpit Voice Recorder

Records conversations on the flight deck and exchanges with air traffic control.

The CAMs (Cockpit Area Microphones) pick up other sounds including the pitch of the engines from which accident investigators can determine their speed of rotation.

With CVRs now a fact of life, it is difficult to believe they were once opposed by pilots' unions as unwanted spies in the cockpit, just as pilots are now resting the introduction of cockpit video recorders which is high on the NTSB MOST WANTED LIST.

In some countries such as Canada, there is legislation to try to ensure recordings of the aircrew's conversations are privileged and not public. This has resulted in the incongruous situation of Montreal Airport being told it cannot use CVR evidence in its defense against Air France. The reason given for granting such a privilege in the first place is allegedly that pilots would not talk freely if they knew their words might be used to their detriment, and therefore might resort to sign language. Perhaps, all the more reason for having cockpit VIDEO recordings as well!

Data Mining

Data mining is the sifting by computer of large quantities of data using Algorithms to pick out trends, abnormalities or signs of particular outcomes. It is used in all sorts of domains including intelligence gathering (i.e. TIA—Terrorist Information Awareness Program), business and industry.

In aviation, it has shown its worth as a means of predicting failures in the absence of obvious signs of anything being amiss.

The greatest problem with data mining is that 'little details' insignificant on their own, but revealing in the context of hundreds of aircraft or events, may not be thought worth recording in the first place. This may be particularly true where human factors are involved. Unlike engineering and maintenance data, these cannot be automatically downloaded.

D. B. Cooper

While not on a par with the legendry Amelia Earhart mystery, that of a fortyish man with receding hair who boarded a Boeing 727 in the United States on November 24, 1971 (under the name Dan Cooper) has likewise been the subject of numerous books and articles. He hijacked it and parachuted from it in the middle of a storm by deploying the rear airstairs with US$200,000 in ransom money. Because of a storm, the fighters trailing the aircraft could not see where he had jumped, making the search for him or his body very difficult.

It is said to one of the most famous crimes in American history, with the FBI interviewing some one thousand suspects, and even recently trying to apply DNA techniques to the case. The man is referred to as *D. B. Cooper* because the first suspect had that name, and the media seized on it, and continued using because it is more mysterious than Dan Cooper, which happens to be that of a French-Canadian comic book hero pictured with a parachute on a magazine cover.

Although he had asked for unmarked notes, they were all notes issued in San Francisco with numbers that were easily identifiable. Despite the offering of significant rewards to anyone finding one, not even one was ever found in circulation, strongly suggesting D. B. Cooper did not survive the jump. A boy found some of the notes some time later but it seems they had been carried down various rivers from elsewhere.

In the area where he is supposed to have jumped, D. B. Cooper became something of a folk hero, with trinkets on sale, and this is possibly why the piqued authorities put so much effort in trying to find out who he was and what happened to him.

DC-8 (Douglas DC-8) [1959] 556

Douglas, the US airlines favorite supplier of airliners was wrong-footed by Boeing when it produced the 707 when other makers including Douglas were expecting there would be an interim period between piston-engine airliners and jet-engine airliners filled by cheaper to run but unromantic turboprops. Once the 707 entered service, Douglas whipped its people in action to get their DC-8 approved by having numerous models for the approval process with the FAA.

Though Douglas had lost sales due to its initial leisurely approach, the 707, despite being famous and doing much to promote international air travel, was not particularly profitable because the arrival of the DC-8 on the scene forced Boeing to incorporate a number of costly design changes to compete. Attesting to the qualities, such as little more space for freight, of the DC-8, is the fact many more DC-8s than 707s have remained in service.

DC-9 (McDonnell Douglas DC-9) [1965] 576 (prior to MD- variants)

The DC-9 was a short- to medium-range twin-engine engine airliner similar to the British BA-11, which had a 2-year lead, but whose sales were to attain only half those of the DC-9. With its engines at the rear, the DC-9 had very clean lines—its fuselage having much in common with the DC-8.

With it evolving into the MD-80, MD-90 and then the Boeing 717MD-80, MD-90 and Boeing 717, the grand total attained almost 2,500 units. Thus, it can be said to be one of the most successful airliners ever.

DC-10 (McDonnell Douglas DC-10) [1971] 386
KC-10 (McDonnell Douglas KC-10 [1981] 64 including KDC-10

Three-engine airliner destined for the medium- to long-haul wide body market in competition with Lockheed's TriStar.

Now viewed as a very safe aircraft following modifications and liked by pilots, it was developed in a rush, and involved in a number of accidents, some scandalous, that gave it a bad name.

See Airbus for the situation at the time, and the narratives in *Air Crashes and Miracle Landings* for further details and narratives.

Early on, a super-DC-10 had been envisaged, but never realized due to the accidents and various downturns in the aviation business. Finally, a derivative was developed, and called the MD-11.

The KC-10 is an airborne refueling platform derived from the DC-10-300.

Deadheading

Refers to crew (pilots or flight attendants) travelling on a flight to reposition themselves to take up duties elsewhere. Not to be confused with *off-duty* personnel enjoying one of the perquisites of working for an airline—free or discounted air travel.

Although the analogy is not strictly correct, the term deadheading is said to be derived from the practice in the theater world of filling up empty seats with non-payers (called deadheads) to give a better ambience. Term also applied to airport tractors without trailers, and even empty railway trains being repositioned.

Dead-Stick Landing

Landing with no power available from the engines. Term evokes leaden feeling of the aircraft controls (joystick in the old days).

Deceleron

A control surface combining airbrake and aileron functions, with the panels split into sections.

Decision Height

Height on an ILS (Instrument Landing System) approach at which the pilots must decide to either pursue the approach with the intention of landing or engage in a missed-approach procedure. Each runway will have its standard missed approach procedure to avoid the risk of the aircraft subsequently wandering into the paths of other aircraft.

Decision Speed V_1

Pilots can only abort their take-off up to the point on the runway where the aircraft attains the so-called take-off *decision speed, V_1.* Thereafter they have to pursue the take-off regardless. This is less daunting than it appears, as the aircraft by then should be able to take off safely even in the event of an engine of a twin-engine aircraft failing. The intention is to avoid pilots aborting the takeoff with insufficient runway remaining for them to bring the aircraft safely to a halt.

Decompression (loss of cabin pressure)

Depending on the rate at which air pressure inside the cabin falls, this can be *gradual, rapid,* or *explosive,* again depending on the height of the aircraft and the nature of the failure that allowed air to escape.

The effects on passengers of *gradual* decompression can be similar to those of failure to pressurize after takeoff, as was sadly the case in 2005 when a Helios Airways 737 climbed to cruising height on autopilot and flew on to its destination (and a mountain) with the pilots unconscious through hypoxia. They had mistaken the aural warning for something else for which it was also used.

In general, gradual decompression is not serious from a safety point of view, and passengers have the benefit of oxygen from their overhead oxygen masks, which automatically drop when cabin pressure falls to that equivalent to 14,000 ft. The limited amount of oxygen provided by these masks is enough to give the pilots time to bring the aircraft down to about 10,000 ft, being careful not to dive so quickly that the aircraft breaks up!

The difference between what is called *rapid* and *explosive* decompression is more a matter of outcome, in that what starts as rapid decompression may trigger explosive decompression, and subsequently the breakup of the aircraft or severe damage leading to complete loss of control.

Fortunately, as narrated in *Air Crashes and Miracle Landings,* lessons have been learnt from some notable explosive decompression incidents such as

- The de Havilland Comets where the fuselage failed.
- The Turkish Airlines DC-10 where a cargo door blew out and the cabin floor buckled downwards damaging vital control lines.
- The Japan Airlines 747 where the uncontrollable aircraft flew around drunkenly for 30 minutes with passengers writing their Wills on their boarding passes after the rear bulkhead failed causing the tail to be blown off.

- The Aloha Airlines where a *flap* in the fuselage structure designed to allow air to escape on failure duly *opened* but failed to achieve its purpose of releasing the pressure because the aperture was blocked by the body of a flight attendant who had been lifted upwards by the gust of air. As a result, much of the cabin roof blew off. The 737 was able to land—minus the hapless flight attendant—with the passengers exposed to the elements as if they were on a London open-top sightseeing bus. Only the rails along the cabin floor for attaching the seats prevented the aircraft from breaking its back.

Simple measures to equalize pressures in the event of a failure in one section—such as incorporating vents and panels between compartments, and say between cabins and the cargo holds below—have greatly reduced the potential consequential risks associated with explosive decompression. It is surprising that it took some serious disasters to force manufacturers and airlines and the authorities to insist on such measures.

Defense News/Defense Contractors
http://defensenews.com/static/features/top100/charts/rank_2007.php?c=FEA&s=T1C
The above page on the website (defensenews.com) of the U.S. magazine *Defense News,* listing the World's top 100 defense contractors, should be particularly interesting to journalists as it dispels the confusion between overall sales volume of the companies and the defense component.

For 2006, it showed Lockheed-Martin in the top spot as regards defense revenue with Boeing not far behind. However, as Lockheed's revenue from defense represented 91% of total revenue compared with 50% for Boeing, its total revenue was less than two-thirds that of Boeing.

Britain's BAE is surprisingly high up on the defense revenue list at Number 3, but then 93% of its revenue came from defense work. EADS, of which Airbus is a major part, is Number 7, but with only 25% of its revenue being from defense its total revenue was twice that of BAE.

Japanese companies are way down on the list, and many U.S. and European companies must be thankful that the Japanese Constitution—dictated very much by the U.S. after the War—forbids the exportation of armaments and their revenue from defense therefore represents domestic sales.
Defense News has much interesting information besides.

Deicing (Anti-icing)
Even a slight layer of snow or ice on a wing can change the way it behaves and drastically reduces the amount of lift it provides. As a result, the aircraft may have to be deiced by spraying with a hot deicing fluid before takeoff and even return to be deiced again should the wait in for takeoff in cold snowy conditions be prolonged. Though the essential ingredient is the same (ethylene glycol or more usually the less toxic propylene glycol), deicing

fluids often contain thickening agents so they form a gel on the treated surfaces for longer protection, in which case they may be called anti-icing fluids.

Deicing is relatively costly in terms of labor and product, and is not good for the environment though attempts are being made to find alternatives to the products currently in use.

Once the aircraft is airborne and fast moving, vulnerable and critical areas can be warmed enough by various means to prevent icing.

Departure

Airline flights are allocated take-off times called slots. If the aircraft misses its slot—perhaps because one or two bewildered passengers are late getting to the gate—the subsequent delay may be considerable. Take-off after missing a slot may depend not only on waiting for another turn at the airport in question but also on getting re-permission to use congested airspace thousands of miles away. Some people are amazed that the estimated time of arrival (ETA) given at take-off invariably proves right on certain long distance flights. This is partly because on some routes, air traffic controllers divide the route into blocks and there is a preset time for entering and leaving each block. In addition to increasing safety, this means aircraft do not bunch up and fly around wasting valuable fuel circling in holding patterns at the end of the journey.

Depleted Uranium (DU)

With a density of more than one and a half times that of lead, depleted uranium is sometimes used where material of extremely high density is required. Its use is controversial because of the incidental risks to human health that may even affect people outside its sphere of application.

Apart from its well-publicized use in munitions—by virtue of its weight and also (in armor-piercing rounds) by virtue of keeping sharp when disintegrating and catching fire once inside (the tank), its civilian uses range from radiation shielding in medical equipment to providing ballast for the keels of sailboats (yachts).

In airliners, it has been used as a counterweight to attenuate vibrations in certain parts of aircraft. Early Boeing 747s in the 747-100 series could have as much as 1½ kg (3 lbs) of DU, much of which was incorporated in the outboard engine nacelles to prevent a nasty flutter at high speed. When, as described in *Air Crashes and Miracle Landings*, an El Al 747-100 crashed into a block of flats in an Amsterdam suburb in 1972, the finding of the presence of uranium added to the suspicions associated with the incident where the aircraft said to be carrying flowers had on board a precursor for nerve gas. The fear was that on vaporizing in the ensuing fire, this could have harmed people, but there was no apparent evidence of this.

Designations (US military aircraft)

As the letter B in aircraft designations (such as B-17) for bombers often designed or made by Boeing can lead to confusion, it may be useful and interesting to explain the main designations. The aircraft mentioned are only examples.

- A -- (Attack) A-10 Warthog
- B -- (Bomber) B-17 Flying Fortress (WWII)
- C -- (Cargo transport) C-5 Galaxy
- E -- (Special electronics) E-3 Sentry
- F -- (Fighter) F-15 Eagle
- O -- (Observation) OA-10 Thunderbolt
- P -- (Maritime patrol) P-3 Orion
- R -- (Reconnaissance)
- S -- (Anti-Submarine Warfare) S-3 Viking
- T -- (Trainer) T-38 Talon
- U -- (Utility) U-2 Dragon Lady
- X -- (Experimental/Research) X-15
- D -- (Drone control) DC-130A
- H -- (Search and rescue) HH-60 Jayhawk
- K -- (Tanker) [The "K" stands for Kerosene] KC-135 Stratotanker
- L -- (Cold weather) LC-130H - ski equipped C-130H
- M -- (Multi-Mission) MH-53E Sea Dragon
- Q -- (Drone) QF-106A - remote control equipped F-106A
- V -- (VIP/staff transport) VC-137C - presidential C-137C transport
- W -- (Weather observation) WC-130J - weather reconnaissance C-130J

    A letter suffix may specify a particular variant of an aircraft such as the F-16A, F-16B, F-16C, and F-16D Falcon

Information partly from: http://www.globalaircraft.org/definitions.htm

Detent

Term often used in connection with flight deck controls, where it is desirable that they can snap to certain positions that can be physically sensed while activating them, thus avoiding the need to painstakingly line up markings. Throttle detents, such as *idle detent* and *takeoff detent* often feature in the aviation context.

Detent should not to be confused with (political) *détente.*

DGAC: Direction Générale de l'Aviation Civile
The French equivalent of the FAA.

Dihedral

For stability, most civilian aircraft wings are dihedral—that is their wings slope upwards as they go outwards from the fuselage like a prized-open letter "V".

When the aircraft rolls to one side, the lower wing is almost horizontal while the other wing points significantly upwards. The resulting difference in effective angles of attack means the lower more horizontal wing produces more lift so the aircraft automatically rights itself. It is a misconception that the greater area of wing facing downwards is what rights the aircraft.

Direct Flights

Many passengers assume so-called *direct flights* are *non-stop*, when in fact the term only means they are on the same aircraft with any number or stops or worse still on different aircraft with just the same **flight number**.

Directed Energy Weapons—Ray Guns

An article in October 30, 2008 edition of *The Economist* (U.K.), http://www.economist.com/science/displaystory.cfm?story_id=12502799, pointed out that ray guns may finally be *about* to become a reality and that they might be used

- for cheaply triggering explosions from a distance
- for destroying incoming artillery rounds and missiles at short range
- for destroying enemy missiles at long range during the boost phase (when they are moving slowly and emitting easily detected heat)
- for purportedly attacking enemy vehicles and matériel at short range on the ground—it being politically sensitive to acknowledge enemy troops (who might boil) would be the main target.

The more demanding applications such as the destruction of missiles at long range would use chemical lasers that can be much more powerful than electrical ones.

Disinsection (sic)

Co-exposure to the tricresylphosphates found both in engine oils and many hydraulic fluids which can contaminate cabin air may make people unusually susceptible to the pyrethroids found in insecticides.

Fortunately, routine in-flight/pre-arrival disinsection (sic) of aircraft with flight attendants walking up and down the aisles spraying insecticide over peoples' heads is virtually unheard of these days, apart from cases where there has been a severe outbreak of say malaria. However, some countries and notably Australia insist on *residue disinsection* (of the aircraft!) prior to the boarding of passengers. See Aerotoxic.

Dispatcher

In the U.K. sometimes referred to as the Airside Business Manager, which indicates the breadth of functions involved, in addition to his or her primary concern, which **should be aircraft safety**.

In the U.S., the dispatcher has to be FAA licensed, and is

Authorized by the FAA to delay, divert, or cancel a flight if not satisfied that it is safe,

and has to sign the dispatch release, which is an official legal document.

Tasks include preparing the flight plan and establishing the maximum allowable takeoff and landing weights, fuel requirement, and so on and so on, taking into account the weather and field conditions. Has to have the knowledge of a pilot coupled with the people-handling qualities and calmness required to cope with the myriad problems that invariably crop up and may delay an aircraft's departure.

In the U.S. and Canada, the dispatcher's work, in theory, includes keeping an eye on the progress of the actual flight, whereas elsewhere, this function is often performed by others.

Displaced Threshold

For various reasons—the presence of high buildings near the beginning of the runway or weaknesses developing in the first part of the runway due to the impact of recurrent landings there over the years—aircraft may be required to LAND further down than they normally would. Since the point just beyond which aircraft would normally land is called the *threshold*, this point further down is called a *displaced threshold*.

Aircraft TAKING OFF can use the zone prior to the displaced threshold, and it can be used for rolling out after landing.

Distances

In drawing up flight plans distances are measured as those at a height of 32,000 ft.

Diversions, Air Rage & Medical Emergencies

Aircraft always carry extra fuel so they can divert to alternates should it be impossible to land at their destination for reasons ranging from bad weather to a terrorist alert. In addition, they may be obliged to divert en route due to engine failure or a sick or deranged passenger.

Diversions are inconvenient and costly, but many an accident has been avoided by doing so, and many an accident caused by failing to do so.

Despite the help usually available, passengers and especially senior citizens, do die in the air. This is especially true of routes such as those between the U.K. and Australia where aged grandparents endure one of the longest journeys in the world to visit their emigrated children and their subsequent offspring. To cope with this, Singapore Airlines have a special locker to place a dead body when no empty row of seats is available.

British Airways lacks that facility, and in 2007, a first class passenger traveling between Delhi and London woke up to find a dead body from Economy Class had been placed at the end of his row, and to make matters worse (for him) two relatives had come along to wail for the remaining hours of the flight. Surprisingly, BA initially offered him no compensation, maintaining he had an attitude problem and should show more respect for the dead!

Diversion Airport

In preparing their flight plan, pilots and dispatchers enumerate the diversion airports (called alternates) situated en route and near the destination to which the aircraft can divert. This could be for any number of reasons, including a passenger falling sick, a technical fault, and particularly bad weather at the destination. See ETOPS.

DMC: Display Management Computer

DME: Distance Measuring Equipment

In conjunction with appropriate equipment in the aircraft, DME beacons can give pilots readout of their distance from them; and even give groundspeed and ETA.

In essence, the beacon is a transponder and replies to an interrogation by the aircraft with the corrected delay indicating the distance. Note that the distance indicated is the slant distance (hypotenuse). Thus, if the aircraft is right above the beacon, the distance indicated will be the height above it!

DNIF: Duties Not Involving (Including) Flying

Acronym used by the U.S. Department of Defense for the situation where pilots are grounded for medical reasons in the very broadest sense.

DOC: Direct Operating Costs

Immediate operating costs, not taking into account other factors complicating the picture. The purchase of fuel is a simple direct operating cost that is easily calculated. On the other hand, in the case of *maintenance*, there is the direct cost of performing the task, and the more diffuse costs and benefits in terms of aircraft availability, reliability, and even safety, dependent on it being performed in a timely manner or even managing it so well (by sophisticated monitoring) that less maintenance is needed.

Dogfight

This term for aerial combat exemplified by encounters in the Battle of Britain in World War II (before the introduction of air-to-air missiles able to launched from a distance) derives from the fact that dogs are said to try to get on each other's tails when fighting.

Doppler Effect

Phenomenon whereby something coming towards one has a higher frequency than when going away—used to be explained to children in terms of the varying pitch of a railway train's whistle when passing at high speed through a station. The Red Shift of stars traveling away from Earth would be another example.

Applied in conjunction with radar, the Doppler Effect can instantly show the speed at which the aircraft is approaching or separating from an object such as the ground. Ground Proximity Warning Systems (GPWS) depend on the phenomenon to determine dangerous sink rates and weather radar can use it to determine movement rates of droplets. Thus can detect wind shear in the presence of rain, but useless for clear air turbulence. See Lidar.

Downwind Leg

See Traffic Pattern.

Drag

Resistance to the forward motion of the aircraft through the air due to friction and displacement of the air molecules.

Drift

Phenomenon whereby the (side) wind blows the aircraft laterally from the direction in which it is heading (pointing). The resultant course over the ground is its Track.

Drip Pricing

Though not restricted to the airline industry, the technique of quoting a low price up front when people are placing a booking online and then adding extras at the end is notorious in some cases. Not only might extras be added on (drip-by-drip) for choice of seat and checking in luggage, a notorious airline might added a significant charge for payment by even debit card on the basis of per person per leg. Thus for a family of four on a cheap trip away, it would mean two legs (there and back) per person multiplied by four making a multiple of eight. If the charge were $5, that would mean $40 extra. The airline would surely make just one transaction costing relatively little. Apparently, by the time people have gone to the trouble of going through the booking routine all the time dreaming of their holiday they find it very difficult psychologically to pull out at the end.

Drug Testing (Random)

Although few in number, high profile cases where pilots under the influence have been taken into custody when an aircraft was about to depart from the gate have led some airlines to resort to testing random urine samples taken from staff flying their routes.

According to the London *Times*, the British company Cozart is supplying drugs-testing kits to Virgin Airlines and Emirates Airlines. These can detect such drugs as alcohol, cannabis, cocaine, amphetamine and heroin. Virgin, for example, apparently used to think pilots would keep an eye on each other, but found that in practice it was too much to expect a pilot to wreck a colleague's career for minor transgressions that were unlikely to represent any real danger.

Dutch Roll

An oscillatory roll-cum-yaw where the aircraft yaws and rolls to one side until the dihedral effect of the wings brings it back to center line, only for the same course of events to be repeated in the other direction.

This unpleasant phenomenon usually results from insufficient directional stability. Interestingly, the cure may not only lie in providing greater directional stability but also in having computer software provide suitable control inputs to preclude the phenomenon developing. As mentioned under Anhedral, computers can even make intrinsically unstable military aircraft appear stable. One of the airbuses found to have a mini-oscillatory problem (a kind of flutter) was cured very simply with the help of a German software programmer.

In the case of what was to become the worst single-aircraft airliner crash ever, a Japan Airlines 747 staggered around for half an hour minus its tail fin to provide directional stability. As the elevators were not functioning to control the pitching, a pitching element was added to the Dutch roll, resulting in a Phugoid roll. See author's *Air Crashes and Miracle Landings*.

Dryden Flight Research Center (NASA)

NASA's Flight Research and Atmospheric Flight Operations Research Facility situated at Edwards Air Force Base in the western Mojave Desert (California).

The facility makes a great contribution to aviation, including in the areas of cockpit displays and safer navigation. See Intelligent Flight Control System (IFCS).

EADS: European Aeronautic Defence and Space Company

European aerospace and defense giant registered in the Netherlands. Embracing Aérospatiale-Matra (France), Construcciones Aeronáuticas/CASA (Spain) and DaimlerChrysler Aerospace/DASA (Germany).

Greatest contribution to sales is from Airbus, with the U.K.'s BAE having sold it share to concentrate on the U.S. market.

Notable EADS product ranges are Airbus aircraft, the Eurofighter joint venture, Eurocopter, the Airbus A400M military transport and the Ariane rocket.

EASA: European Aviation Safety Agency

http://www.easa.europa.eu

European Agency based in Cologne, Germany (established in 2003 and only now operational) responsible for safety matters, with actual regulatory power as opposed to the JAA (Joint Aviation Authorities) which preceded it. First major act was the certification of the Airbus 380. See JAA.

EasyJet

A very successful British low-cost carrier (LCC).

Helped by

- Having purchased aircraft at greatly discounted prices during industry slump;
- By recently introducing highly professional management;
- By recently being able to tailor its early morning and late evening departure times to suit business travelers.

While its rival, Ryanair, flies to airports situated sometimes a long way from major city centers, easyJet flies to many airports likely to suit business people. A sophisticated software program, allegedly with as many as 14 different fare levels for each flight, enables it to maximize profit, while taking care not to overdo the milking to the detriment of the brand.

According to the French magazine *Capital*, on a typical flight only 10% of passengers may be paying the advertised cheapest fare; and even though some passengers may be paying as much or more than they would have on airlines such as Air France, the *easyJet* brand's reputation for being cheap is so strong that passengers fly with them regardless. Like its immediate rival, the company's lowest fares are subsidized by the fact that passengers quite often book them on a whim and do not turn up for the flight allowing the airline to keep the surcharges such as airport tax which can in many cases be many times the so-called fare.

It seems that easyJet had noticed how, over the years, airlines purchasing Airbuses had seemed to receive favorable treatment with regard to traffic rights to France. Apparently, they expected similar largesse when they recently purchased Airbuses while simultaneously seeking to take over slots about to become available at Paris on the failure of some French airlines operating there. They duly bought the Airbuses—reportedly at very good prices due to Airbus wanting to break Boeing's stranglehold on the low-cost airline market—but ended up with the Airbuses without the slots, perhaps because they prematurely consummated the marriage. Was what they were hoping for too detrimental to French interests anyway?

ECAM: Electronic Centralized Aircraft Monitor (Airbus)

A system that keeps an eye on all systems and presents pilots with information in order of urgency, with Chimes as appropriate. First introduced on the A320, where computer control had been something of a revolution, and then in other Airbus craft.

Boeing's equivalent system is called EICAS.

Echelon

An arrangement for the gathering and pooling of communications intercept intelligence by the U.S., the U.K., Canada, Australia and New Zealand. Tapping into connections used to be relatively easy when many communications were via simple cable, satellite and microwave links. Now with fiber-optic cables and VoIP (Voice over Internet Protocols) such as Skype, this is less true, and less easy to see who is talking to whom.

Other countries have similar systems, with business intelligence a profitable vein for all.

EFCS: Electronic Flight Control System

EFIS: Electronic Flight Instrument System

Though kept as backups, the traditional electro-mechanic instruments are being replaced by mostly LCDs (Liquid Crystal Displays) that have the virtue of being able to show much more information in one place and different sets of information on a given screen at the turn of a knob or the pressing of a button.

EICAS: Engine Indicating & Crew Alerting System (Boeing)

A display usually situated above the throttles showing complete information about engine performance, fuel management, and alerting pilots of system malfunctions even including airframe failures. Should a malfunction occur, pilots receive an aural alert with not only the *screen* for that part of the system automatically coming up, but also a list of corrective actions. Part of the EFIS (Electronic Flight Instrument System).

Airbus have an equivalent system called ECAM.

Ekman, Professor

See Behavior Detection Officers.

Electra (Lockheed Electra)

Name given to two distinct airliners

- **(1) Electra 10 [first flight 1934] 149**

  10 seats, with slightly smaller or larger variants

Used by many airlines and by the military in WWII.

Specially adapted version used by Amelia Earhart with extra fuel tanks in the place of seats. See *Air Crashes and Miracle Landings*.

- **(2) L-188 Electra [1958] 170**

  was a very promising fuel-efficient turboprop airliner seating up to 92 passengers in the economy configuration.

  Early accidents limited sales prospects. Once rendered very safe, it was too late, as the public had come to believe that pure jets were intrinsically better than turboprops.

  It was largely due to bad luck that Lockheed got its fingers burnt as the two most dramatic accidents were due to vibratory harmonics (flutter) at high speed that no one could have predicted at the time and which were easily dealt with once known.

Electronic Flight Bag (EFB)

The electronic flight bag is not a bag in the traditional sense, but an electronic device replacing the increasingly voluminous paper documentation (Aircraft Operating Manual, Aircrew Operating Manual, Navigational Charts, Airport Plans, etc.) that pilots lug around in their carry-on bags. One of their great advantages is the ease with which they can update material—without the need to substitute paper pages with the updated ones.

In addition, pilots can use them to calculate fuel requirements, rotation speeds, and so on. The latest versions can incorporate moving airport map displays with own ship position indication that could almost halve runway incursions and virtually eliminate such tragic errors such as the case where a Singapore Airlines aircraft took off from that disused runway at Taipei.

Elevation

The elevation of a point is its height above mean sea level (msl) as opposed to height above the surrounding terrain (agl). On charts for airmen, the elevation of high points (say buildings near an airport) are given, with the height above the surrounding terrain (agl) in parenthesis underneath.

Elevon (Elevator + Aileron)

Instead of having elevators (in the tail) to solely control pitch, and ailerons in the wings to solely control rolling (banking), some aircraft such as the late supersonic Concorde with its delta wings have the two combined at the wing trailing edge. If both go up or down together in equal amounts they act as elevators; if the amounts differ, they act like ailerons; and of course, any combination of the two is possible. However, the input from the pilot remains traditional (as if elevators and ailerons were separate) with complex mechanisms, or more often now computers, producing the simulation. There are even *Flaperons*, combining flaps and ailerons, but applications using these are limited.

EMAS: Engineered Material Arresting Systems

Rarely installed, but highly effective bed of specially engineered sand-like material beyond the end of a runway into which the wheels of an overrunning aircraft sink deeply enough to rapidly slow it but not so sharply that it flips over. In the 100-MPH Qantas overrun at Bangkok described in detail in *Air Crashes and Miracle Landings*, the water-laden soil performed similarly and certainly prevented a major disaster. Some military fields have arresting wires or nets that can be flipped up when needed—especially important considering the nature of some military payloads.

Emerging Technologies

These are fledgling technologies that seem promising but often need a lot of development work, and not least trial and approval from the authorities. An example would be SHM.

Emirates

See Connectors.

Empennage

The empennage is the Tail Assembly of an aircraft.

Derived from French where it meant the tail feathers of an arrow. Depending on the aircraft, empennage includes the vertical stabilizer & rudder and horizontal stabilizer & elevators. The empennage is often prominent in news photos of crashed aircraft with the airline's logo obvious, leading some airlines to attempt to have it painted it out to avoid bad publicity. See Ruddervators.

Endurance

The number of minutes the aircraft can theoretically stay airborne with the fuel on board.

Engine Maker

An increasingly used term to distinguish the engine manufacturer from the aircraft manufacturer increasingly referred to as *Airframer*.

Engine Stall

See Compressor Stall.

Envelope/pushing the (flight) envelope

The *flight envelope* is a high-sounding but useful expression meaning *that which is within the boundaries of what the aircraft or space vehicle can sensibly be expected to be capable of in controlled flight.*

There can be some confusion regarding its use as test pilots can be said to be pushing the flight envelope to prove what the aircraft is capable of, and designers can be said to be pushing the envelope with the design improvements they make regarding normal flight.

Engineers can tag it onto certain words to indicate specific aspects of the envelope, such as airspeed envelope or altitude envelope.

EPR: Engine Pressure Ratio

Indicates thrust generated by Turbofan Engines. However, with most of the thrust produced by modern high-bypass turbofan engines coming from the fan, N1 and N2 are often seen as more significant indicators of thrust.

ETOPS: Extended-range Twin-engine OperationS

With engines becoming increasingly reliable, twin-engine aircraft are (under certain conditions) being allowed to fly routes taking them a long way away from airports suitable for landing in an emergency.

The civil aviation authority of the country where the airline is registered is responsible for approving ETOPS flights and only does so when fully satisfied that the aircraft is suitable and that the airline's maintenance procedures are beyond reproach. Revocation or limitation of the scope of their ETOPS approval is a constant threat overhanging small airlines relying on them for their operations. They have to report engine shutdowns and the authorities are on the watch for any sign of lax maintenance procedures. This theoretically might lead some airlines to pressure pilots into avoiding shutdowns or precautionary diversions that would flag-up their maintenance problems. Thus, a policy adopted to promote safety can as is often the case have the opposite effect

Interestingly, some experts are arguing that having exceedingly reliable engines means more emphasis should now be placed on other factors, such as a passenger falling sick, how long cargo hold fires can be contained and problems with the fuel where the number of engines is irrelevant. Some ask whether there should be provision for extra clothes for flights where the aircraft might divert to some Polar airfield. A Virgin Atlantic aircraft not so long ago diverted to such an airfield because a passenger had a heart attack, and in the course of taxiing in icy and unfamiliar conditions clipped a wing on something on the side of the runway. As a result, the passengers had to remain for a time at a cold location with very limited facilities.

EUCARE European Confidential Accident Reporting

System based in Berlin for the confidential report of incidents. Similar to CHIRP for the U.K., and ASRS for the U.S.

EuClaim

http://www.euclaim.co.uk/

The European Union has brought in rules to (try to) force airlines into paying compensation for cancelled flights except when due to a *force majeure* beyond the airline's control.

A recent *Dispatches* TV program on U.K.'s Channel 4 cited the cases of BA passengers seeming to receive standard letters refusing them compensation on the grounds that crew were not available/used up, even though it might have been 6:30 in the morning, due to exceptional circumstances.

For the individual passenger or party this is obviously very difficult to disprove, and here the Dutch lawyers (Euclaim) have stepped in with a clever system:

> By analyzing departure delays for European airlines using data from diverse sources they can identify cases where cancellations are routine, and obviously not due to exceptional circumstances but failure to engage sufficient staff or for economic reasons.

> Their site even has a *Claims Calculator* that can help people see whether they might have a potentially viable claim of up to £470 per passenger.

While British Airways may baulk at the prospect of paying compensation to passengers in Coach (Economy), some Business Class travelers regard them as a soft touch, making all sorts of overblown claims about poor service in the hope of getting upgrades or free tickets.

EUROCONTROL

Despite its name, EUROCONTROL is not an EEC institution but an autonomous organization originally founded in the sixties by Belgium, France, Germany, Luxembourg, the Netherlands and the United Kingdom to control upper air space. It has evolved with other countries, and even the EEC itself, signing up.

Essentially, it deals with ATM (Air Traffic Management) but has other roles particularly concerned with safety and the management of databases.

Evacuation, Emergency

As mentioned under the entry 90 Seconds, certification tests must show that the totality of the passengers must be able to evacuate in that time.

EWD: Engine Warning System

Explosion-Suppressant Foam (ESF)

See Ullage.

Extension (Runway Extension)

A somewhat confusing term used by controllers to mean not the physical runway itself but an imaginary line projecting beyond its end. Relevant where a taxiway passes close to the end of the runway and might be hit by an overrunning aircraft. Term used by the controller in the *meandering Cessna disaster* at Milan's Linate Airport.

FAA: Federal Aviation Administration (U.S.)

The body responsible for supervising airlines, aircraft certification and air traffic control in the U.S. Sometimes has a difficult balancing act between safety concerns and the commercial interests of the airlines and aircraft manufacturers, in contrast to the *purer* NTSB, which investigates accidents and only makes recommendations. Many countries rely on the FAA for the certification of aircraft and much else and could be said to be having a free ride. However, as the aircraft and much of the equipment used are often U.S.-made, the advantages are not all one-way.

FADEC: Full Authority Digital Engine Control

Just as on the engines of modern high-performance cars, the control systems on modern aircraft engines have to consider so many factors and adjust so many parameters to achieve maximum efficiency that only a digital computer can handle the task.

The point has now been reached where engine control may be completely automatic with the pilots unable to intervene regarding particular aspects. As a breakdown of the control system could render an engine useless, the systems are usually in triplicate. Though the systems are engineered to allow for extreme power requirements in an emergency there is a point beyond which they will not go—to protect the engine.

The systems also provide data for maintenance.

Fallacies

According to NASA's Glen Research Center *Aerodynamics Index*, many of the theories propounded in books and encyclopedias as to how airfoils (aerofoils) produce lift are downright wrong or only partially valid. In fact, the way wings and even winglets work is more complicated than first thought, and designing them is something of an art.

The first of some four or five fallacies cited is

- *Equal Transit Theory* sometimes called the *Longer Path Theory*, which claims: that as the path of the airstream over the wing is longer than under the wing, and that, as the two airstreams must leave the wing at the same time, the one over the wing must be travelling faster. Hence, the latter must be at a lower pressure due to the Bernoulli Effect, and that it is this lower pressure that, according to the fallacy, produces the lift.

See
http://www.grc.nasa.gov/www/K-12/VirtualAero/BottleRocket/airplane/wrong1.html

They say that another fallacy is that ground effect is primarily due to an aircushion formed under the aircraft keeping it up, whereas the aerodynamic scenario is much more complex.

FAR: Federal Aviation Regulations

Regulations classified under relevant headings (Parts) covering every aspect of aviation, including the operation of flying schools, operation of ultralight vehicles (such as trikes), certification of pilots and aircraft. Points to note are that although the regulations are constantly updated, once an aircraft is certified it does not lose it certification even though it might not do so under subsequent regulations—though there are limits to this.

In view of the time and cost involved in getting new designs certified, manufacturers can be tempted to continue with less than the best—even say for cockpit instrument layout.

Fares

In the immediate post World War II years when national flag carriers ruled the roost with their government's support, international airfares were fixed at high levels with IATA managing the system. The system began to break down with airlines covertly selling seats in parallel at considerable discounts through so-called 'bucket shops'. Nowadays deregulation means pricing is something of a free-for-all.

However, the doubling of fuel prices has recently on occasions led to fuel accounting for as much as 40% of an airline's operating costs and airlines are seeking all sorts of ways of procuring extra income and reducing those costs.

Extra income sources include charging extra for phone reservations, hold luggage and credit card payments. According to U.S. aviation consultant Robert Mann, fares based on passenger weight might be the next logical step. Most think this would be difficult or impossible. However, Southwest Airlines in the U.S. has managed to achieve this partially by asking passengers to buy a second seat if their girth prevents the armrest from lowering. Of course, charging according to weight would be a two-edged sword as light-weight people now subsidizing others could demand to pay less.

Fashion (rear-mounted engines)

It was once the fashion to have engines mounted at the rear of the aircraft, partly to reduce cabin noise and partly because would theoretically give a cleaner more efficient configuration. Now the fashion is to have the engines in pods under the wings, which makes servicing easier and facilitates the installation of the new super-powerful large diameter engines. One disadvantage of high-tail/rear-mounted engine configurations is that the tail drops in a stall making it difficult, if not impossible, to recover.

The rear engine configuration was once much favored by Russian designers.

Fasteners

Usually a rivet, bolt or screw for fastening items together, which sounds very mundane, but a term that Boeing has highlighted in explaining the manufacturing problems it has been having with their new 787. First, the necessary fasteners were in short supply, and now it seems some such as those for attaching composites to titanium were fitted incorrectly, with corrective work perhaps entailing the use of larger fasteners (hence heavier) to fill the holes already made.

Fatigue (human)

As terrestrial drivers of cars and trucks have found, fatigue is a major cause of accidents and is on the NTSB's Most Wanted LIST.

Fatigue (metal)

See Cycles.

FCDC: Flight Control Data Concentrator

FCL: Flight Crew Licensing

FCMS: Fuel Control Management System

FCOM: Flight Crew Operating Manual

FCPC: Flight Control Primary Computer

FCSC: Flight Control Secondary Computer

FCTM: Flight Crew Training Manual

FD: Flight Director

FDR: Flight Data Recorder

Records the last half hour or so of numerous aircraft parameters permitting accident investigators to more easily determine what happened. FDRs are getting more and more sophisticated, with modern ones sometimes referred to as DFDR (Digital Flight Data Recorders).

One problem is the so-called sampling rate, in that say the position of the rudder is recorded at intervals (several seconds) with no indication of how it moved in the meantime. This made it more difficult to see what happened when the copilot apparently swished off an Airbus tail on encountering wake turbulence after taking off from JFK.

Ferry Flight

A non-revenue flight to position the aircraft for a subsequent flight or to take it back to home base or other location for maintenance. Sometimes an airline might carry out such a flight with no passengers to keep its right to a valuable landing/takeoff slot.

Environmentalists criticized BA in 2008 for flying an empty 747 from London to Hong Kong. The airline claimed it was because they could not muster the required cabin crew—if the airline had another flight to Hong Kong that day and few passengers, it might have been cheaper to put all on the one aircraft. Not all is what it seems.

Statistically, non-revenue flights (as a whole) are more likely to be involved in accidents than passenger-carrying revenue flights.

Fin (tailfin): Vertical Stabilizer (U.S.)

Fixed vertical aerofoil on tail, usually with the (movable) rudder inset that as the U.S. name for it implies keeps the aircraft directionally stable (i.e. stops it yawing).

Final/Final Approach

Final leg of the descent, leading straight to the runway. There is also the term *late final* meaning less than two nautical miles from the runway.

FIR: Flight Information Region

FL: Flight Level

Flame Out

Once started, a jet engine has a flame that burns continuously. If for some reason, such as lack of fuel or ingestion of foreign substances (debris), the flame goes out, the engine will no longer produce any power. Flame out rather than stop is the term used as an engine will usually continue to rotate after a flame out due to the wind milling effect.

To prevent the flame from being blown out by a sudden gust of air, engines incorporate a *flame holder* in the form a small cusp that behaves like the cusped hand used to light a match in a strong wind.

Flaps

Panels at the rear of the wings that tilt downwards at various angles (and usually also extend backwards thus increasing the area of wing) to give increased lift at slow speeds such as when taking off and landing.

An aircraft with amazing flaps was the Boeing 727 where the wing almost seemed to double in width as they extended, with one being able to see right through it in places. This enabled the aircraft to use small airports, but the tremendous potential sink rate meant unwary pilots sometimes could not recover in time. Early versions of the 727 required 45% power just to maintain altitude at the full flap setting.

Flare (Landing Flare)

Just before the aircraft touches down on the runway, there is the *flare*, which is rather similar to what an eagle does—rather more ably when alighting on a rock by opening wide (flaring) its wings and rearing up just before its claws touch.

The aircraft flare initiated at a height of about 50ft and fully realized at a height of about 30ft, consists of raising the nose so that the extra lift slows the descent. However, with the engines not supplying any significant thrust, this decrease in rate of decent is only transitory as the extra drag produced by the increased Angle of Attack reduces the airspeed so much that the aircraft can no longer stay airborne and sinks onto the runway.

Flight Attendant

William Milberg's fascinating *Famous Airliners* tells how in 1930, Ellen Church, a nurse and flight enthusiast, suggested that Boeing Air Transport (BAT) have nurses on board to look after the passengers. At the time, some European airlines had male stewards, but on BAT, one of the pilots would give out the sandwiches. With her as BAT's Chief Stewardess and employing seven other equally young nurses, a trial was held despite reservations of many higher-ups at the airline. The nurses proved extremely popular and letters poured in praising them, and thus a *new profession was created.*

As airliners became more comfortable and began to fly at heights where turbulence was not usually a problem, the need for comforting by nurses became less evident. In addition, managers had discovered that with the increased number of passengers per aircraft, they usually had medical and nursing services on tap in the form of the rich doctors and even nurses that statistically would be among the passengers. Another advantage was that the usually expensive professionals called to help could hardly demand payment without looking mean.

From 1950 onwards there followed a period during which in some countries, the *air hostess* as female flight attendants were then called, was portrayed as a glamour girl to lure (male) passengers to the airline. Advertising became highly suggestive, including photos of provocative girls with captions such as National Airlines' *Fly Me!*

Fears grew that selecting female cabin crew for their beauty and cuteness risked compromising safety. Japan Airlines, with its female cabin staff being somewhat on the dainty side, had to introduce a test involving stepping up and down a high step 50 or 100 times to confirm their cabin crew were physically strong enough to cope with the physical demands of an emergency requiring the opening of doors and so on.

With some notable exceptions, this romanticizing of the flight attendant came largely to an end, as union pressure and anti-discrimination legislation, especially in the U.S.—some say unfortunately—have gradually removed many of the strict conditions such as age limits and body weight previously imposed.

In the U.K., cabin crew can now *in theory* be taken on even up to the age of 62 (compared with 30 in the 1970s), thus giving them 3 years until the mandatory retirement age of 65! The term flight attendant began to replace *airhostess* and *stewardess*, though it is said the term *cabin crew* is now favored in recognition of their safety role.

Indeed, cabin crew and notably females, perhaps because they are more numerous, are well documented as having saved lives through their powers of observation, quick action and courage. Cases in point are the discovery of the Shoe Bomber, the calming of crazed passengers and ensuring the safe evacuation of passengers from burning aircraft.

Flight Data Management (FDM)/Analysis (FDA)

The analysis of data gathered for specific flight so lessons that can improve safety can be learnt. Obligatory in some countries, but not in the U.S. (where it is known as Flight Operations Quality Assurance (FOQA)) due principally to pilots fears as how the information might be exploited. See Data Mining.

Flight Deck (Cockpit)

For better or worse, airliner manufacturers are increasingly designing *cockpits* for two-man crews. Technology simplifies control and checking, and is thought to have rendered the presence of an expensive third human in the role of flight engineer unnecessary. The literally hundreds of dials that used to litter cockpits are being replaced by screens that at the turn of a knob or the push of a button can show various sets of data.

This represents quite a change from the first 747s that had almost a thousand lights, switches, and gauges on the flight deck, and which certainly needed the attention of a dedicated engineer!

Even so, very long-haul flights often have a reserve pilot or reserve pilots to permit the others to have the occasional rest. The reserve might or might not be qualified to carry out take-offs or landings in bad visibility for example. This matter of what pilots are not legally allowed to do but might actually be capable of doing has sometimes been cause for unnecessary alarm where cabin crew have inadvertently scared passengers by announcing their pilot is *unable* to land the aircraft when they simply meant he lacked the qualifications for the weather conditions!

However, leaving less qualified/experienced pilots to handle the aircraft during supposedly quiet periods does have its downside in that they may be flying in Coffin Corner where everything seems fine, but can go terribly wrong as perhaps happened in the case of Air France Flight 447.

Flight Director: FD

One step above the Autopilot, it tells the autopilot what it should do based on input from the pilots, the Flightplan loaded into it, terrain databases, and navigational data provided by GPS and radio beacons. See Autopilot.

Flight International/Flightglobal.com

Flight International is the name of the paper edition of the highly respected U.K. aerospace magazine.

Though it can be highly critical of even the major players in the aviation world, like all such publications regularly carrying full-page ads for such players, it seems not to pursue exposés regarding them single-handedly, which would do little to increase their readership anyway. Investigative reports in say the *New York Times*, *Herald Tribune*, the French *Le Monde*, the German *Der Spiegel*, and elsewhere, can be more provocative, and even they have to worry about being sued.

The Flightglobal.com website is a valuable gateway to much information and even videos.

Flight Level (FL)

When aircraft are high up with no danger of hitting the ground but still in danger of hitting each other, air traffic controllers assign them flight levels with the unit being in 100 ft. Thus Flight Level 1—which would never be used!—would mean an *altitude* of 100 ft, while Flight Level 250 would mean 25,000 ft.

A standard barometric altimeter adjustment of 1023.2 millibars (29.92 inches of mercury) is used for flight levels so that aircraft at the same altitude will have same altimeter reading.

In some countries, such as Russia, China, and Mongolia, flight levels are given in full in meters, with no division by a factor such as 100.

In addition, there are rules regarding the assignment of flight levels, so that aircraft do not fly, in say opposite directions, at the same flight level. See Altimeter and Holding Pattern.

Flight Plan

An official document filed with aviation authorities prior to departure listing details of the flight (names of crew, number of passengers, destination, waypoints, speeds, alternate airports, etc., etc.).

A flight plan may not be legally required the case of general aviation flights under VFR, but it is usually advisable to file one so rescuers know where to start looking if the aircraft is reported lost. The crashed GA aircraft of millionaire adventurer Steve Fossett only found by chance months afterwards is a case in point—he had not submitted a flight plan.

Flightplan (in one word) is the name of a thriller movie starring Jodie Foster where a woman's young daughter disappears midflight with the captain and crew believing she is hallucinating and the daughter never came on board.

Florian Trojer (aviation photographer) http://floriantrojer.com

Prize-winning aviation photographer, whose possession of a commercial pilot's license enables him to go that extra distance. Typical of his artistic touch is the picture of an airliner climbing out from Innsbruck airport, with a towering snow-capped cliff alongside, used on the front cover of *Air Crashes and Miracle Landings*.

Flutter

Vibrations that can build up in an aircraft's structure due to flexing and the generation of harmonics, and possibly lead to its destruction, with this sometimes referred to as flutter. Adjusting distribution of masses and degrees of rigidity are some of the methods used to preventing its occurrence. Suitable computer software programming for control inputs can often curb nasty tendencies without resorting to structural changes or adding weights.

London's Millennium Bridge over the River Thames is an example of the phenomenon. Nicknamed the *wobbly bridge*, it had to be closed only a few days after its official opening for corrective measures due to serious wobbling in harmony with pedestrians' footsteps.

Fly America (policy)

This is the obligation for Federal employees and contractors to fly on American airlines or book through the U.S. code where a U.S. airline has a code share agreement with a foreign airline. It is a bone of contention in negotiations regarding landing rights and so on.

Flying Cheap

A program on the U.S. PBS TV channel entitled *Flying Cheap* looked into the situation at Regional Airlines following the fatal crash on February 12, 2009, of Continental Connection Flight 3407 operated by the Regional Carrier, Colgan Air.

FM: Flight Management

FMGEC: Flight Management, Guidance Envelope Computer

FMS: Flight Management System

See Autopilot/Flight Director for details of systems to which the Flight Management System can give orders.

When people say *pilots have nothing to do these days* and that the autopilot can fly an airliner from London to Hong Kong without their help, they really should say the Flight Management System.

This system is based on two main elements:

- Databases
- Flight Plan

The databases hold navigational data about terrain, air routes, waypoints, navaids, restricted areas, height restrictions, runways, and engine performance data enabling the FMS to determine takeoff distances, optimum speed and height according to weight of fuel remaining together with other data.

The flight plan is loaded into the system prior to departure with details of amount of fuel, all up weight and temperature together with all the other necessary information such as waypoints, destination, and so on. It can be set up manually, but for regular routes would be all or in part a standard one for the flight in question.

FOD: Foreign Object Damage/Foreign Object Debris

Damage from foreign objects such as something on the runway (say something fallen off another aircraft) or in the air such as birds is always of concern—though engines are tested by having (dead) chickens thrown into them to ensure they can withstand a certain amount of abuse.

FPV: Flight Path Vector

Freedoms (Overfly, Landing Rights)

Commercial Aviation Rights negotiated between governments. These negotiations often involved brinkmanship and acrimonious horse-trading between government officials.

Colonial countries such as France and the U.K. could strike good bargains as many countries' airlines wanted to land both in the home country and in the overseas possessions. Few people know that the onetime Crown Colony of Hong Kong was a valuable bargaining chip for the U.K. negotiators as so many airlines wanted to go there.

- 1st Freedom: Pure over-flight rights; no landing except in emergency. Now that spy satellites can anyway see into countries, they tend to be more willing to let foreign airlines overfly their territory.
- 2nd Freedom: Right to land for refueling and maintenance without transfer of passengers or freight.
- 3rd & 4th Freedoms: Right to take passengers and freight to the other country and back respectively. Usually granted together.
- 5th Freedom: In addition to 3rd and 4th Freedoms, right to carry passengers from one's own country onwards to a third country.

One subcategory (Beyond Fifth Freedom) permits carriage of passengers from second country to third country, while the other subcategory (Intermediate Fifth Freedom) allows passengers from third country to be transported to the second.

- 6th Freedom: Right to use one's own country as a transit point or hub to transport passengers or freight from a second country to a third, say between Australia to Europe via Singapore or Bangkok.

- 7th Freedom: Right to carry passengers or freight between two foreign countries without involving one's own.

- 8th Freedom: Right to carry passengers or freight within a foreign country in the context of service on to one's own. Also called *cabotage*.

- 9th Freedom: Rarely given right to carry passengers or freight within a foreign country without service from or to one's own. Also called *stand-alone cabotage*.

See Open Skies Agreement.

Frequent-Flyer Programs

At first sight, programs whereby passengers can collect *air miles* and gain points allowing them to use special lounges at airports seem a good idea. However, they are anticompetitive in that an airline lucky enough to have slots used by business passengers will almost automatically have numerous members, who will be unlikely to shop around and experiment when purchasing other tickets.

Interestingly, some airlines have exclusive unpublicized clubs for the super-elite.

Fuel (rising cost of)

The rising cost of aviation fuel has been a boon to the aircraft manufacturers by forcing airlines to buy the newer more fuel-efficient aircraft. Some U.S. airlines have 20-year old fuel-guzzlers.

The cost of fuel does particularly affect the viability of ultra-haul routes, as the longer the route, the more fuel that has to be carried just to transport that fuel. From a purely fuel efficiency point of view, legs of just a few thousand kilometers would be cheapest. However, landing charges, personnel charges at stopover points, the need for more pilots and not least the fact that passengers would dribble away to rival operators complicate the issue.

Fuel Reserves

Countries and airlines have strict regulations about the fuel an aircraft should PLAN to have in reserve on reaching its destination to allow for unexpected headwinds or diverting to another airport (again with appropriate fuel reserves)should landing there be impossible. See Re-dispatching.

Funneling (Navigation Paradox)

The sky is a big place and the chances of aircraft hitting each other if flying completely randomly would not be so great in some areas. However, routes and flight levels are not random and now there is the paradox of the danger that as navigational systems such as GPS and even altimeters place aircraft ever more accurately (+/- a few meters) that an error by ATC, or simply confusion regarding long-distance flight rules, will place aircraft at exactly the same spot. It has been calculated that fewer accidents would have occurred over the years had aircraft operated more randomly in certain situations.

While there is the inevitable funneling of aircraft as they come into land, it is not so much of a problem then as ATC are closely watching separation. However, there may be some unnecessary funneling in other situations. Would the tragic mid- air collision over Lake Constance —in the middle of the night with hardly anyone around—of a freighter and an airliner full of children have occurred had the Swiss Air Force not appropriated so much airspace, leaving little room for commercial traffic to roam?

With future ATC systems (such as the FAA's NextGen) being even more precise and depending on trajectory rather than on simple separation on a set path or airway, one wonders whether this so-called Navigation Paradox will be invalidated. See Aircraft-Centric.

FWS: Flight Warning System

"G"

Force experienced by persons or aircraft due to gravity and/or acceleration or deceleration. Expressed as a multiple or fraction of the Earth's gravitational force.

Negative-G refers to the situations where the aircraft drops or accelerates downward so suddenly that there is a feeling of weightlessness. See Bunt.

GA: General Aviation

Especially in the U.S., refers to aircraft operations and aircraft that are neither military nor commercial (where commercial means scheduled airline flights).

This sector thus covers anything from the flying club Piper Cub, through business jets, to unscheduled cargo and unscheduled airliner operations. In practice, the business jets and unscheduled cargo and airliner operations flying into and out of major airports are supervised very much like commercial flights in contrast to most GA operations in and out of small airfields where regulations are less strict.

According to Wikipedia, the British Business and General Aviation Association interprets it to be *all aeroplane and helicopter flying except that by the major airlines and the armed forces.*

On the other hand, the ICAO defines GA as *an aircraft operation other than a commercial air transport operation or an aerial work operation,* with *commercial aviation* defined in the very broadest sense, which is too wide for most people.

Gait analysis/Facial recognition

Everyone has heard about *facial recognition* where computer programs are used to (try to) identify people from still images or frames from CCTV cameras. There are even plans, for example in the U.K., to use it at passport control. Not many have heard of *gait analysis* whereby people are identified from the way they walk—which is surprising considering we very often recognize relations or friends in a crowd from the way they walk.

Interestingly, some thought is being given to recognizing people from above, say from satellites or drones, by converting their horizontal shadows to show their gait. While this might work in sunny Pakistan or Afghanistan, it would not be much use in the U.K. with its cloudy weather. The program would have to be able to recognize those trying to alter their gait by putting a stone in their shoe.

Geared Turbofan (GTF)

Pratt and Whitney, part of United Technologies, has invested considerable funds ($1bn) in the development of the so-called *geared turbofan* engine. Sophisticated planetary gearing enables the front fan to operate at a different speed from that of turbines in the rear section. This is theoretically advantageous, as fans—such as the large diameter rotating blades one sees at the front of aircraft engines—are more efficient at low speeds, which in turn allow greater fan diameters, whereas turbines are more efficient at high speeds. Having both operating at optimum speeds should allow higher bypass ratios and a more efficient, cleaner fuel burn and quieter operation.

The geared turbofan has already been chosen to power the new Bombardier 135 C series regional jet and for Mitsubishi's new airliner.

Competitors have expressed (hopefully?) some doubts about whether Pratt and Whitney's gearbox concept will be reliable and about the ongoing cost of maintenance, while pondering the wisdom of their own strategic choices.

General Aviation (GA)
See GA.

-Generation (e.g. Fifth-Generation)

Both in the field of computers and aircraft (notably fighters) the Fifth-Generation at the moment seems to indicate the most modern generation as regards the technology. In the case of fighters, there was a Generation 4.5, where there was no great technological leap on the aerodynamics front, but where great advances were made in electronics and avionics. Now there is talk of a 5.5-Generation.

GKN: Guest Keen & Nettlefolds

GKN is a British company with a very long history starting in Wales in 1759. Once was vertically integrated in that it produced upstream steel and coal and downstream products such as fasteners and railroad rails. Now tries to concentrate on sophisticated downstream products, and uses only the initials GKN as its name.

The company has purchased the Filton factory near Bristol that makes the wings for Airbuses. (The research center remains the property of Airbus.)

Glide Path

Imaginary path, aligned with the runway and at an angle of about 3° leading to the touchdown point on the runway.

See ILS (Instrument Landing System) and VASIS.

Glide Ratio (fuel depletion/engine failure)

Indicates how far an aircraft can fly without engines and is simply the distance gained forwards divided by the height lost, or the forward speed divided by the sink rate, or the cotangent of the downward angle (one can calculate back the angle). It is also called the *lift-to-drag ratio* (L/D), which is the term more normally used for powered aircraft (not intended to be gliders) as an indication of the efficiency of the airframe.

Gliders (sailplanes) can have glide ratios approaching 60, whereas modern airliners have glide ratios (L/Ds) around 16-18.

There have been two remarkable cases, described in *Air Crashes and Miracle Landings* where airliners have been able to glide considerable distances after fuel depletion occurring at cruising height and effect safe but hard landings.

GNSS: Global Navigation Satellite System

Go Around

The term go-around simply means the pilots decide to abandon the landing for some reason, such as a poor approach due to gusty winds, wind shear, bad visibility, or perhaps because an aircraft taking off from the runway they intend to land on has taken more time than the air traffic controller expected.

Airliner controls have a TOGA (Takeoff-Go-Around) button. Pressing it automatically reconfigures the aircraft and resets the throttles for an immediate climb away.

Since the computer is programmed to think a TOGA input situation may be an emergency, say to avoid an aircraft still on the runway, the resultant maneuver is somewhat abrupt and liable to scare the passengers. Consequently, some pilots perform the go-around manually when they think the situation permits. Often the passengers will come back telling stories how they missed another aircraft by a few feet, when it was just a precautionary action, taken well before landing when the controller finds the aircraft having already landed is taking longer than expected to exit it. To nervous passengers, banks, turns, and climb outs can seem steeper and more dangerous than they actually are. This is also because not being on the flight deck they cannot anticipate them as they would in a motor vehicle.

GPS: Global Positioning System

A navigation system, now well known as SatNav to the public. Location, speed and direction of travel of the aircraft are determined by tracking three or more satellites with a special receiver.

Originally developed for U.S. military but offered free to the public following the shooting down of a Korean Airlines 747 that had supposedly lost its way. It used to have potential inbuilt errors to stop enemies using it to guide missiles and so on, but that faculty is not now employed—at least in times of world peace. New techniques enable GPS destined for the public to be locally degraded in war zones.

To increase accuracy and not least to confirm readings are accurate at a time when users are increasingly dependent on the system, supplementary systems are being introduced. These work by having ground stations monitor the satellite signals and broadcast corrections to make the positioning accurate enough say to land an aircraft.

In the U.S. they are the WAAS (Wide Area Augmentation System) designed to cover most of the country and LAAS (Local Area Augmentation System) designed to cover particular areas such as those in the vicinity of airports. The European's have their EGNOS (European Geostationary Navigation Overlay Service) based on satellites, while the Japanese have their MSAS (Multi-Functional Satellite Augmentation System).

Interestingly, a GPS-based system called PTC (Positive Train Control) is being developed in the U.S. for preventing train crashes by plotting their positions, noting their speeds and warning them of the risk of collisions—and applying the brakes should drivers fail to take appropriate action. It incorporates a WAAS type system, called Nationwide Differential Global Positioning System, to increase accuracy to about a meter. With train crashes less feared than air crashes, railroad companies are reluctant to install it widely despite the fact that it would raise average speeds and allow trains to pace themselves thus saving fuel. Plane and train come together. See ADS-B.

The Europeans are developing their own GPS system called Galileo to which the Chinese and other countries are signing up. Russia and China also have their own systems with limited coverage. The new Russian system called GLONASS was initially developed (like the original U.S. GPS) for the military, but will be made available for public use.

GPWS: Ground Proximity Warning System

With hindsight, a no brainer (obviously needed) system for warning pilots when they are inadvertently too near the ground, and one that has done more than any other to prevent CFIT—controlled flight into terrain. It was made mandatory for large aircraft in the U.S. in 1974.

Using the data fed anyway to the radio altimeter giving actual height above ground, it gave a verbal warning if the aircraft was dangerously near the ground, sinking at a rate making it difficult to recover in time, and so on.

Readers may have heard cockpit voice recordings of crashes ending with the GPWS warning PULL UP! PULL UP as the aircraft is about to hit the ground.

Early versions would sometimes give too many spurious warnings, resulting in it being switched off in countries where at the time it was not mandatory. A case in point was the French Air Inter Airbus A320 flight into Mont St. Odile in 1992 where the GPWS system had been deactivated because pilots claimed there were too false alerts.

The great drawback of the original system was that it could only warn pilots if the ground immediately below was dangerously close, and not if they were about to fly into a mountain or cliff lying directly ahead. However, there are now enhanced versions where radio altimeter data is complemented by data about the terrain ahead derived from a worldwide terrain database and identified by coordinates provided by GPS (SatNav).

Grandfathering

In the domain of regulation and certification, getting an improvement approved by say the FAA is costly and involves time-consuming and expensive trials and procedures. Thus, even a modification that is obviously an improvement as regards safety over an approved system with latent dangers may not be implemented. Even after crashes due to these latent dangers, the FAA has been prone to resolve the problem by merely accepting modification of the operating manual.

Graveyard Spiral and Spatial Disorientation (SD)

Mention of the term *graveyard spiral* brings to mind the fatal disaster that befell the light aircraft the late President Kennedy's son, John F. Kennedy Jnr., was piloting over water at night with his wife and sister-in-law as passengers.

Investigators found nothing wrong with the aircraft, engines or equipment on recovering the aircraft from the bottom of the ocean. It was thus presumed that Kennedy became disorientated due to not being able to see the horizon, allowed the aircraft to bank until it entered a graveyard spiral where, with the aircraft already tipped on its side, pulling back on the controls would only further tighten the spiral and cause the aircraft to drop even more precipitously.

When disorientated and unable to see the horizon, a pilot should rely on his instruments to tell him the attitude of the aircraft or remove his hands and feet from the controls and rely on the autopilot to extricate his predicament.

In Australia's *The Sunday Age*, aviation medicine expert Dr. David Newman is quoted as saying *80% of a person's sense of what is up or down is determined by sight and with the remaining 20% determined in equal share by vestibular (ear) and seat-of-the-pants sensations.*

The trouble is that the latter sensations can be confusing when combined with G forces, while vestibular sensations are subject to drift like that affecting gyroscopes, but over a period of seconds rather than hours. Thus, spatial disorientation easily comes about when pilots cannot see the horizon, with it being claimed it is more likely to occur when pilots do not have much to do.

Pilots are trained to cope with it by the instructor putting a mask over their eyes so they can only see the instruments, confusing them by executing various maneuvers and then getting them to redress the situation using only the instruments. Even so, it is said that quite a number of the general aviation accidents that do occur are due to SD, which can even make pilots feel they are sitting on the wing!

Ground Effect

Depending on the type of wing—the supersonic *Concorde* with its delta wing perhaps being a prime example—an aircraft can get extra lift and show greater efficiency when close to the ground. Some believe it is rather like a cushion of air pushing the aircraft up when in fact the aerodynamics are much more complex than that.

There have been cases, say when an aircraft has had ice on its wings reducing their effectiveness, where the ground effect has allowed the aircraft to become airborne, only for it to fall back when gaining height.

When *Amelia Earhart* took off from Lae in her overloaded Lockheed Electra on her fatal final flight, the ground effect was what just enabled her to get into the air.

Ground Speed (as opposed to Airspeed)

True speed over the ground, as opposed to the speed through the air.

Passengers do not always realize that a 50 M.P.H. headwind would mean they would be going 100 M.P.H. faster the other way. This is why aircraft can sometimes fly non-stop one way but not in the other direction.

Gyro & Gyroscope

Gyroscopes are constantly spinning tops in special bearings that allow them to maintain their orientation regardless of that of the aircraft. In the simplest form there is the directional gyro which when set according to the compass gives the magnetic bearing. Advantage over the pure magnetic compass is that readout is steady. Over time, gyroscopes drift and give inaccurate output. See Inertial Navigation.

Hand off, to hand off

A term used in air traffic control, where aircraft are *handed off* from one ATC facility to another.

Recently, the phrase appeared in the media when a Delta Airlines flight coming into JFK was handed off from the FAA's traffic control center in Westbury, N.Y., to the Kennedy tower, and finding they did not have the right frequency for communications with the tower, the crew quite rightly decided to effect a go-around. In so doing, they came somewhat too near to an aircraft taking off from a perpendicular runway. In consequence ATC procedures at the airport are being revised—the pilot's decision to go-around being normal.

Heading

The heading is the direction in which the aircraft is pointing, as opposed to the aircraft's Track over the ground, which is affected by the wind direction/velocity. See Crabbing where the aircraft is pointing to one side but tracking in line with the runway.

Head-Up Display (HUD)

Not everyone realizes it is simply what it says it is, namely a display that permits the pilot to see pertinent information on the windscreen while looking out of it with his or her head up.

With increasing degrees of sophistication, HUD systems can be

- **Basic Systems**

    With symbolic information such as height, heading, airspeed and so on displayed using special symbols.

- **Enhanced Flight Vision Systems (EFVS)**

    With also an enhanced view of the terrain ahead obtained via an infra-red camera situated close to the pilot's line of sight so that on coming out of the clouds the view will be the same;

- **Synthetic Vision Systems (SVS)**

    With a computer-generated view of the terrain ahead derived from databases.

HUDs were originally developed as gun sights.

Headwind/tailwind

In many parts of the world, the prevailing winds are from West to East, and hence around-the-world balloon attempts are made in that direction. What is sometimes forgotten is that a headwind when flying in one direction will be a tailwind for when flying in the opposite direction and that this greatly increases the difference between the flight times for the two directions.

"Heavy"

Heavy is a call sign suffix (e.g. United three-two-one *heavy*) that indicates to air traffic controllers the presence of a large aircraft requiring more space (separation minima) than lighter craft. Heavy is defined as an aircraft that has a gross takeoff weight greater than 255,000 pounds in the U.S.A and greater than 300,000 pounds in some other parts of the world. This includes the larger aircraft in use today. However, some aircraft are on the borderline, as their takeoff weight can depend on their seating configuration and other factors. One aircraft that can have it both ways is the 757 according to its load; however, it is invariably referred to as *heavy*, in that it is notorious for producing nasty wake turbulence.

Helicopter

Answers to questions many ask about helicopters can be found at http://www.helis.com/faq/.

Helicopter blades incorporate a freewheeling mechanism allowing the blades but not the engine to freewheel. In other words, the engine drives the blades but the blades do not drive the engine—as a result if the engine fails, the blades will continue to rotate and prevent the helicopter dropping like a stone. However, to keep the freewheeling blades rotating and enable the helicopter to make a controlled landing without engine power, it is desirable that the helicopter have at least some forward speed and is one reason why some news organizations instruct their pilots to keep moving around rather than remain hovering for extended periods when filming incidents.

That said, helicopters are nowadays very reliable—the spare parts are expensive—and incidents of engine failure rare. Incidents are more likely where the much greater convenience of travel by helicopter in certain situations tempts people to take risks in bad visibility.

While the helicopter excels by being able to take off and land vertically, it also has to be able to move horizontally, and this is not too much of a problem at low speeds.

As the forward speed increases the fact that the advancing blade is travelling through the air faster and the retreating blade is travelling more slowly becomes significant, and would make the craft unstable. A procedure called *flapping*, whereby the pitch of the blade when retreating is higher than when advancing is used to compensate for this. However, there comes a point, where speed of the rotor on the retreating arc equals the airspeed with the result that lift on that arc is completely lost, and a further increase in forward speed would even result in negative lift. Even before reaching that point, the pitch changes would be too great. Thus, the maximum speed of a helicopter is inherently limited.

So-called Tilt Rotor helicopters combining the advantages of the helicopter with those of a fixed wing aircraft can travel much faster, but suffer a lift penalty as the wings partially obstruct the down draft from the rotors. The rotors tilt through 90°, so that in normal forwards flight the fixed wing provides all the lift.

HF: High Frequency (radio)

High-Bypass Turbofan Engines

Modern commercial airlines' jet engines are much quieter than the screaming versions prevalent in the 1960s and 1970s. This is partly achieved by having the turbines at the back of the engine drive an enormous fan at the front that blows air to the back with much of it bypassing the combustion section, Hence the use of the word *high-bypass*.

Holding Pattern (Stack)

When aircraft cannot land at an airport because others are already waiting to land, bad weather and so on, they are put in a queue but as they have to keep moving to stay in the air, they are stacked up in rectangular patterns, usually in the vicinity of a VOR beacon. Each aircraft will be at a different Flight Level and will drop down to the next level when told to do so by ATC.

Howard Hughes

Legendary figure whose very real contributions to aviation are sometimes overshadowed by his glamorous early life involving film stars and his later eccentricities.

The movie, The Aviator, portraying his life, well shows the run-ins he had with a senator protecting the interests of Pan Am's Juan Trippe. Hughes took a very personal interest in the cockpit layout and other aspects of Lockheed's Constellation.

HSI: Horizontal Situation Indicator

Horizontal Situation means location with horizontal reference to points on the ground. Can be set in ILS/VOR/NAV indication modes.

Hub-Buster

New term for ultra-long range versions of an airliner, such as the Boeing 777, making it possible to fly ultra-long routes with a full load without refueling at the customary intermediate hub. Particularly applicable to routes to Australia and New Zealand. However, the rise in the cost of fuel is making this an expensive option, as the extra cost of carrying that tremendous weight of fuel begins to outweigh by far the savings in time and charges at intermediate airports.

Human Error

With the great improvements in technology and materials and the greater reliability of turbine engines as opposed to piston engines, human error now represents an increasingly large proportion of accident causes. This is not to say human performance is worse. In fact, with CRM and so on, it is improving, but that other factors are less significant now thanks to improvements in many areas.

Hydrogen-Powered Airliners?

Some have suggested that airliners could burn hydrogen produced by nuclear power-generated electricity and thus be non-polluting as all they would produce would be water. One drawback is that hydrogen has a much lower energy density than the kerosene now employed.

Hydrostatic Shock

Bullets (from guns) penetrating the body at very high velocities cause damage well beyond the point of entry and trajectory due to a phenomenon called hydrostatic shock. Mentioned in *Air Crash and Miracle Landings*, in the context of the .303 shot that brought down the Red Baron.

IALPA: International Airline Pilots Association

IATA: International Air Transport Association

Airline trade organization based in Montreal, Canada.
At one time, with many carriers being national airlines (flag carriers) governments gave them dispensations under anti-cartel regulations to fix fares through IATA and even colluded themselves.

However, now with deregulation, the body is doing much useful work.

ICAO: International Civil Aviation Organization

United Nations agency responsible for aviation matters based in Montreal Canada but not related to IATA, which is also based there. Has seven regional offices. Sets many international norms.

IED: Improvised Explosive Device

Because the abbreviation is short and can mean anything from a hollow-shaped charge able to blow up an armored vehicle to a big firecracker destined to sow panic, it is widely used by official bodies such as the U.S.'s TSA to describe any improvised (homemade?) explosive device—i.e. anything other than standard munitions.

IFE: In-flight Entertainment (Systems)

In-flight entertainment systems allowing passengers to watch movies have become very important as one of the ways to make journeys less disagreeable and seem shorter.

In view of the amount of wiring required, the use of Wi-Fi to transmit the data required for flight entertainment systems has been very seriously considered for the latest aircraft, but has encountered two obstacles. The first is getting approval from the official international body controlling such matters for a special intra-aircraft waveband. However, it should finally be realized. The second is that with more and more demands being made on the systems, Wi-Fi may finally not be able to provide the necessary bandwidth.

IFF: Identification of Friend or Foe

The first Transponders were IFF devices to tell radar operators in World War II whether aircraft were friend or foe.

IFPS: Initial Flight plan Processing System

IFR: Instrument Flight Rules

Situation where poor visibility or Air Traffic Control requires the pilots fly according to the air traffic controllers' instructions and their instruments rather than visual observations of landmarks. Pilots have to be suitably qualified. See VFR.

ILFC: International Lease Finance Corporation

In terms of fleet value, the world's largest aircraft leasing company. HQ is in Los Angeles.

Attempts to sell it off in view of the plight of its parent company, AIG Insurance, may succeed, assuming a strong enough entity such as a sovereign fund takes up the challenge. Problems at ILFC could affect Boeing and Airbus sales, and the terms governing the rescue of AIG mean that financing terms for aircraft will not be as favorable as before.

ILS: Instrument Landing System

A system, whereby two radio beams (one in a vertical plane for the glide-slope and the other in a horizontal plane as the horizontal localizer) create an artificial glide path and tell pilots (or the aircraft autopilot) whether they are above or below the glide-slope, or to the left or right of the projected centerline of the runway.

In good weather, the pilots can make a visual approach, with the VASIS lights near the touchdown point changing color to provide similar but less critical information.

IMC: Instrument Meteorological Conditions

Visibility below that stipulated for flight under VFR meaning that flight only permissible under IFR.

Mentioned in connection with Air New Zealand flight that was "programmed" to crash into Mount Erebus in Antarctica, in that the pilots thought visibility was good enough for them to fly under VFR.

Inertial Navigation System (INS)

Before the advent of GPS, inertial navigation used to be the key to navigation in isolated places with no navigational aids. Also used for guided missiles (ICBMs).

Although less accurate than GPS, it will still operate if satellites are not functioning or jammed in time of war. Essentially, consists of gyros for determining direction, and masses supported by sensors for determining acceleration and deceleration. On aircraft, three independent systems are used so if one malfunctions the malfunctioning one (the odd one out) can be identified.

The Korean Airliner (KL007) shot down by Russian fighters would have been using INS. Allegedly, that incident led to President Reagan giving permission for the civilian use of GPS.

"Infant mortality"

As explained under *Bathtub Curve*, the failure rate of equipment tends to be relatively high when new (*infant mortality*) but quickly falls to a very low level that is maintained for a long period (sometimes referred to as *useful life*) before rising on *wearing-out*.

Insulation (Electrical, Thermal, Acoustic, etc.)

Insulation used in the construction of airliners sometimes means insulation used to prevent the propagation of heat (cold) or noise, rather than electrical insulation.

Intelligent Flight Control System (IFCS)

NASA's Dryden Flight Research Center in cooperation with other research centers and institutions has been working on the development of "self-learning neural network (NN) software for aircraft flight control computers".

In its final form, the software would compare data from how the aircraft and its systems are operating with a database of how it would normally operate, and automatically adjust the flight controls to compensate for any damaged or inoperative control surfaces or systems". The BNET business dictionary defines an Artificial Neural Network (ANN) as *an information processing system with interconnected components analogous to neurons, based on mathematical models that mimic some features of biological nervous systems and the ability to learn through experience.*

Recent studies have tried to establish whether an ANN approach could be applied to situations where a pilot is disorientated by being upside down or for other reasons unable to cope.

Intersection (navigation using radio aids/VOR)

The points where Radials from VOR beacons intersect are known points and key elements of traditional navigation. They have identifying codes with those pertaining to an approach to a specific runway incorporating that runway number.

IR: Inertial Reference

ISIS: Integrated Standby Instrument System

ITCZ: InterTropical Convergence Zone

Air France flight AF447 was in that zone, well known for its stormy and fickle weather, when it dropped out of the sky en route from Rio de Janeiro to Paris.

JAA: Joint Aviation Authorities

Body to integrate aviation related regulations in Europe now superseded by EASA.

Member states:
Austria, Belgium, Croatia, Czech, Cyprus, Denmark, Estonia, Finland, France, Germany, Greece, Iceland, Ireland, Italy, Latvia, Luxembourg, Malta, Netherlands, Norway, Poland, Portugal, Romania, Serbia, Slovenia, Spain, Sweden, Switzerland, Turkey and the United Kingdom.

Jane's

Jane's Information Group describes itself as *a world-leading provider of intelligence and analysis on national and international defense, security and risk developments*. Initially famous as a British publisher of books on fighting ships, aircraft and so on, Janes has expanded into the organization above.

One can sign up to receive (free!) weekly emails with tempting mini-extracts from their various publications. Valuable source for latest information on Air Transport, Airports, in addition to Military and Security matters.

Jeppesen

A U.S. company, now owned by Boeing, that over the years has developed into a key supplier of navigational charts and particularly ones required for flights into and out of airports. With worldwide coverage, Jeppesen charts and systems have become something of a standard. The British have their similar *Aerad* flight guide and navigational chart system.

JFK/Kennedy Airport (John F. Kennedy International Airport)

New York's major (international) airport, formerly known as Idlewild (IDL). It is so well known that the public generally refers to it by its code JFK. One runway is almost the longest commercial runway in the U.S., and being at sea level the best for long haul flights.

John Doe Immunity

In November 2006, a group of imams returning from a U.S. Imam Conference was removed from a U.S. Airways domestic flight after a passenger passed a note to the crew reporting their anti-American remarks. Flight attendants had also noted they were not sitting together but dispersed, while two of the party had asked for seat belt extensions although one did not require one.

The following November, a judge allowed the imams in question to pursue their discrimination case, but with the John Does (the passengers who had cast aspersions) no longer cited, on the grounds that the U.S. Congress had in the interim granted immunity to passengers on aircraft reporting suspicions. In the U.S., the term John Doe (like Mr. 'X') is used in legal proceedings when there is no specific name.

Joy Stick

Despite many thinking the term for the upright lever between the pilot's knees used to control the attitude of the aircraft (amongst other things) must be derived from slang, it is probably corruption of *Joyce Stick*. An Englishman called Robert Joyce worked on the development of such a control in the period leading up to the First World War.

While many airliners now have control columns rather than a joystick, it is notable that Airbuses have Side Sticks, consisting of a short control stick to the left and right of the Captain and Co-pilot respectively.

Juan Trippe (June 27, 1899 – April 3, 1981)

Although the name suggests Spanish or Cuban origins, Juan Trippe was actually of Northern European stock. He graduated from Yale in 1921, and after working on Wall Street, founded various airlines and ultimately Pan American World Airlines.

He received many honors before and after World War II. Often credited as one of the great driving forces that made the airline business what it is today. It was Juan Trippe's ability to exploit his connections in high places that enabled him to find funds to purchase small airlines, and subsequently to create Pan Am and expand it internationally with some significant degree of legislative protection. This in turn enabled him to place large orders for aircraft such as the Boeing 707 and 747. However, the financial burden of the latter purchase exposed the international carrier's underlying weaknesses earlier than perhaps otherwise would have been the case. See Pan Am and Howard Hughes.

Judgment Errors

In their book *A Human Error Approach to Aviation Accident Analysis,* Wiegmann and Shappell point out that analysis of over 4,500 pilot-causal factors associated with nearly 2,000 U.S. Naval aviation incidents showed that:

- Judgment errors (e.g. decision-making, goal setting and strategy selection errors) were associated more often with major accidents, whilst procedural and response execution errors are more likely to lead to minor accidents.

Putting it in a motoring context, they compare the former to deciding to run a red light which could result in deaths, and the latter to miss-timing ones braking and causing what in the U.S. is called a fender-bender. Pushing the argument further they say this dispels the widely held belief that the (causal) difference between a major accident and a fender-bender is little more than luck and timing. One should perhaps add the caveat that Navy pilots encounter more situations where decisions are needed compared with airline pilots flying set routes with almost everything dictated by the company.

Kapton

Electrical insulation material used for many years for electric wiring in aircraft. Recently there have been concerns about brittleness with ageing in the case of aircraft over 25 years old. In view of its many pluses, aircraft manufacturers were loathe to change to other insulating materials, as not possible to be sure that any new material might not show similar or even worse problems after 25 years.

Knot (kt): Nautical Miles per Hour

Aircraft speeds are usually measured in nautical miles per hour or knots.
1 knot = 1.853 km per hour, or 1.16 Statute Miles per hour.

LAAS (Local Area Augmentation System)

System being developed in the U.S. for enhancing accuracy of GPS navigation systems in local area around airports, whereby say four fixed reference GPS receivers compare their actual positions with those determined by a satellite fix, and send the differences so detected to a central processor, which transmits a correction by VHF to avionics in the aircraft. It is hoped to achieve accuracies of less than 1 meter, thus permitting Category I, II, and III precision approaches.

LAAS also can immediately detect failure or inaccuracies in the GPS system, perhaps deliberately introduced in time of war.

WAAS (Wide Area Augmentation System) is a similar, but U.S.-wide (as opposed to local) system for improving accuracy. Signal combined with satellite signal and can be utilized by civilian GPS equipment. Other countries, such as Japan and some in Europe are developing their own augmentation systems.

Ladkin, Peter J.

Ladkin is Professor of Computer Networks and Distributed Systems at the University of Bielefeld in Germany. He and his team have done much work on air accidents.

Lady Grace Drummond Hay

This courageous woman had gained her title of Lady by marrying a man fifty years older than she was, and who was to die three years later. Under the sponsorship of the newspaper proprietor Randolph Hearst, and with little experience then as a journalist, the widowed Hay joined a round-the-world voyage in the airship Graf Zeppelin in 1929.

Departing from a location near New York the airship flew to Germany with little incident. Then it flew on to Tokyo, crossing the Soviet Union in cold conditions and with the risk of colliding with high peaks; then on to Los Angeles with the airship encountering a severe storm and believed lost; and finally on to the point of departure near New York to a rapturous reception.

Her reports transmitted from the airship and during stopovers had made her famous, and she used that fame to further the cause of flying and women's roles in subsequent years. Interned during the Second World War by the Japanese in the Philippines with her journalist companion with whom she was at times very intimate, she fell sick after her release and died in 1946. A remarkable TV documentary portrays that round-the-world trip with footage from the actual times.

Landing

This critical part of the flight can be divided into the *Approach, touchdown* and *landing roll.*

- Approaches (including *final approach and late final approach*)

   In approaching the runway, the aircraft follows the Glide Path, which is an imaginary slope, of about 3 degrees, leading to the ideal touchdown point situated some distance beyond the runway threshold to allow a safety margin in case the aircraft lands short. Major airports have radio-wave systems that tell the pilot whether he is on the glide path, and the autopilot may even be able to fly the aircraft accurately down the glide path, and land the aircraft automatically.

   As in taking off, there are certain critical speeds when landing, the main one being V_{REF}, the Reference speed for landing. It depends on various factors but mainly the weight and configuration (i.e. the flap settings) of the aircraft.

   A target speed slightly higher than V_{REF} is chosen to allow for wind shear or gusts. For instance, in the case of the Qantas

Bangkok overrun, the pilots decided on a target speed of V_{REF} + 5 knots because of the blustery conditions. In fact, they came in faster at 19 knots over V_{REF}. (The company limit was V_{REF} + 20 knots, so, as the captain stated, the landing was *just about acceptable*.)

- Touchdown

Just before touchdown, there is the *Flare*, which is rather similar to what a large bird does—rather better—to alight on a rock by opening wide (flaring) its wings and rearing up. The aircraft flare, initiated at a height of about 50ft and fully materialized at a height of about 30ft, consists of raising the nose so that the extra lift slows the descent. However, this slowing of the descent is only momentary as the extra drag with the wings at a greater angle of attack without the engines supplying significant thrust reduces the airspeed so much that the aircraft can no longer stay in the air and sinks onto the runway.

Though passengers tend to clap if the landing is very soft—they should sometimes thank the computer and remember that there are occasions when a hard definitive landing is preferable. This can be when the runway has a layer of water on it, as landing hard makes the tires cut through it rather than aquaplaning. It may also be safer when there is a strong or variable crosswind.

- Landing Roll

To avoid any waste of valuable time and in consequence using up runway unnecessarily, sensors send a signal to the aircraft's computer the moment the tires touch, so that it can immediately apply the wheel brakes and deploy of the spoilers. The *spoilers* are simply the hinged rectangular panels on the top of the wings that can flip upwards to counteract the lifting action of the wings. When flying it enables the aircraft to sink rapidly without the passengers having the uncomfortable feeling of it pointing downwards, or in the case of a landing, forcing it down on the runway so it does not bounce. By putting the full weight of the aircraft onto the wheels, it makes the brakes more effective. The spoilers also have a braking effect when the aircraft is traveling at high speed.

As on the better modern cars, the *wheel brakes* have anti-skid/anti-locking systems so maximum braking is possible, if needed. The degree of braking can be preset, depending for instance, on how far the aircraft has to go down the runway before turning off.

Pilots can also use the engines to slow the aircraft using a system called *Reverse Thrust*. This simply means the thrust of the engines is directed forwards by means of movable cowlings on the engines to give a braking effect. Many readers will have noted an unusual roar from the engines just after landing, which would have been the application of reverse thrust.

The recent introduction of carbon brakes, which wear less when applied continuously and do not fade, means that the most modern aircraft can USUALLY stop quickly even without application of reverse thrust PROVIDED THE RUNWAY IS NOT CONTAMINATED (not icy or covered with standing water). Thus reverse thrust is often engaged in case of need, but with the engines left idling in what is called idle-reverse (thrust).

Lease (Wet/Dry, etc.)

Aircraft are often leased by carriers rather than bought outright. Leasing can take the form of a

- A **Wet Lease** where the Lessor provides (and pays for) almost everything, namely the aircraft, the aircrew(s) and cabin crew(s), maintenance and insurance (hull and third party risk);

- A **Damp Lease,** which is the same, except that the lessee provides the cabin crew;

- A **Dry Lease,** which is essentially a financial arrangement, with the aircraft operated by the lessee as if it were its own.

  A **Dry Lease** can either be

    an **Operating Lease** where the Lessee employs the aircraft for a relatively short period of usually from two to about seven years, and the a/c does not appear on the lessee's balance sheet,

    or a **Financial Lease,** where the aircraft appears on the Lessee's balance sheet and the length of the lease may be three quarters the usable life of the a/c after which the Lessee would have the option of purchasing the aircraft at an agreed price, and so on.

A Wet Lease of less than a month would be called an **Ad Hoc Charter**.

Not only does leasing free up cash. An airline having purchased an aircraft from a manufacturer at a substantial discount *might* be able sell it to a bank at true value thus recording an instant profit and lease it back with payments split over many years. Leasing companies themselves often place large orders thus obtaining discounts and a good place in the queue for coveted aircraft.

LCC: Low Cost Carrier

Airlines such as easyJet, RyanAir and JetBlue offering cheap fares and usually benefitting from the absence of legacy cost structures.

Leading edge

The front edge of something, usually of the wing or tail plane, that meets the airflow first.

Learning curve (aircraft production costs)

From the time of the Second World War, aircraft and other manufacturers have been aware of what they called the learning curve. It is the notion that doubling production reduces production costs by 20%, as staff learn how best to perform their tasks. Since it is easier to double production costs from a small number, this results in a curve that is very steep at the beginning. In fact, aircraft that come off the production line in the very early years are often sold at a considerable loss, even if development costs are averaged over the expected longer run.

This is in addition to extra manufacturing costs associated with certain out-of-the-ordinary projects such as the super-jumbo Airbus A380 or the Boeing 787 Dreamliner employing composites for the fuselage.

This also applies to a lesser extent variants, and manufacturers acceding to too many special demands from clients can fall foul of this and lose money even where the total for a given aircraft seems quite high.

Legacy Carrier

Shorthand, especially in the U.S., for airlines that became bloated in the heyday of commercial aviation where regulated high ticket prices enabled them to pay high salaries and set up expensive facilities for hub and spoke operations. Has negative overtones suggesting this legacy of a high-cost wage structure supported by powerful unions makes them vulnerable to LCCS (Low Cost Carriers) and bankruptcy.

LIFO: Last In, First Out

Term used in computing, accounting and so on which describes how elements in a queue are treated. An example would be a pile of books with the last one to be placed on the pile and at the top being taken off first.

When an airline suffers a downturn in business, it is the most junior pilots (the last to arrive) who are laid off first. Not as bad as it seems, as the pilots that are let go, who may well be better than those retained, may seek work at LCCs and commuter airlines thus meaning those airlines have some very good ones.

FIFO (First In, First Out) would be the reverse. See Age of Pilots.

Lidar : <u>L</u>ight <u>D</u>etection <u>a</u>nd <u>R</u>anging

Term coined in a similar fashion to the way Radar (RAdio Detection And Ranging) was, but where light waves instead of radio waves are involved.

Lidar is a new method using light waves from lasers instead of radio waves to detect turbulence, wind shear and wake turbulence. Lidar also refers to state-of-the- art technology in the aerial mapping domain with accuracies down to 10-15 cm possible.

Lift

Lift is the term used to describe the upward forces generated by the forward motion of the aircraft through the air. An aircraft can suddenly lose lift (Stall) if it flies too slowly or its configuration changes so that the behavior of the air passing over and under the wings suddenly changes. The phenomena involved are much more complex than claimed in some books. If it were that simple, manufacturers would have already designed the perfect wing, and if it were merely the Bernoulli Effect, aircraft could not fly upside down.

LINKS to useful glossaries (also accessible via OpenHatchBooks.com)
FAA Pilot/Air Traffic Controller Glossary

> http://www.faa.gov/atpubs/pcg/

- AirDisaster.com: Definitions

  http://www.airdisaster.com/defs/

- Meriweather: Definitions

  http://www.meriweather.com/fd/def.htmlJerome

  Meriweather's home page is mostly valuable as a gateway to his Flight Deck Simulations [for the 777, 767, 747, A340, A320 & F-16], where clicking with the mouse on an instrument or control produces an explanation of what it does.

- Thirty Thousand Feet™

  http://www.thirtythousandfeet.com/

- ALLSTAR Educational Network

  http://www.allstar.fiu.edu/

  Partly funded by NASA. Ssite for teachers and students at all levels.

- Wikipedia

  http://www.wikipedia.org

- *"Aviation"* in Yahoo's "Directory"

  http://dir.yahoo.com/

- Flight International (U.K.) and flightglobal.com

- Aviation Week (U.S.)

  www.aviationweek.com

- Links for Aircraft Designers

  http://www.aircraftdesign.com/other.html

  "Cool websites for hot designers! Internet Links for aircraft and spacecraft designers, including companies, universities, government agencies, military, professional societies, museums, and private websites. The emphasis is on resources for designers, but includes museums and photo sites as well."

- Aerospace Technology Com

  http://www.aerospace-technology.com/

LNAV and VNAV

Abbreviations for LATERAL and VERTICAL navigation respectively used in cockpit instrumentation. When switched "ON", the Flight Director – Autopilot takes instructions regarding lateral navigation and/or vertical situation (height) directly from the FMS (Flight Management System).

Load Factor or PLF (Passenger Load Factor)

As representing the proportion of airline seats filled and taken to be a good indication of how well the airline is performing.

Not always as meaningful as one might suppose, as it does not indicate the prices at which that capacity was sold. Also taking aircraft out of service increases apparent load factor, and saves on fuel and operating costs, but capital costs and overheads remain.

LOC: Localizer

Horizontal guidance component of ILS (Instrument Landing System) telling pilot where he or she is relative to the centerline leading to the runway—i.e. right on it, or to the left or right of it.

Lockheed-Martin

In terms of revenue from defense-related work, Lockheed Martin is the World's largest defense contractor. See Defense News. The present incarnation is the result of the merger between Lockheed and Martin Marietta in 1995.

When the original company first started manufacturing commercial aircraft in 1912, it was called LOUGHEAD AIRCRAFT MFG. Co. The name was so difficult to read that there were posters telling people to pronounce it *Lock-Heed*.

Around the same time, the Glenn L. Martin Company was founded in Los Angeles. In 1916, it merges with the Wright Company, but in 1917 and with outside backing, Glenn Martin pulls out and reestablishes the Glenn L. Martin Company in Ohio. Lockheed and Martin go on to great things, with the former producing flying boats, airliners and fighters. In 1961 Martin merges with the American Marietta company to form Martin-Marietta, and although the latter's forte was aggregates, cement and chemicals, the stronger financial footing no doubt helped it become a force with which to be reckoned. In 1993 Martin-Marietta acquires General Electric Aerospace for $3bn, thus giving it a footing in the satellite domain, in addition to its already strong presence in the rockets and missiles domain.

One highlight, or rather lowlight, came in 1982 with a hostile takeover bid by the Bendix Corporation. Although Bendix managed to acquire a majority of Martin Marietta shares, Marietta's management in turn managed to use the interim period between ownership and cession of effective control to sell off non-core businesses and to takeover Bendix itself using the so-called Pac-Man Defense. Ultimately, Bendix was sold off leaving a somewhat indebted Martin- Marietta intact.

Despite its glittering history as a maker of civilian airliners such as the pre-War Electra used by Earhart and the elegant post-War piston-engine Constellation, Lockheed later pulled out of the civilian airliner business, deeming it too risky.

This was because the company had lost tremendous sums, more through bad luck than through any failure of its own, when their superior wide-body Lockheed Tri-Star (L-1011) missed the boat in the face of competition from the ill fated, hastily produced, MacDonnell Douglas DC-10.

Lockheed had missed out on sales due to problems Britain's Rolls-Royce had in perfecting the new more powerful engine required and the fact that it subsequently took too long to offer more powerful engines. However, in those days, there were three suppliers in contention in the wide-body market so it was easier for one to fall by the wayside; now there are only two: Airbus and Boeing.

Loiter Time (LT)

A rather appropriate military term for the length of time an aircraft on a mission can stay at the scene:

LT = Endurance – Commuting Time (from & back to base)

Particularly relevant to maritime patrol aircraft, ground/air support aircraft, surveillance aircraft and AWACS type aircraft. There is even now the notion of *loiter munitions* in the form of tiny missiles which would lurk overhead for hours to be directed at the enemy at the opportune moment—their precision (say with laser targeting directed from the ground) means only a tiny warhead would be required.

LSA: Lowest Safe Altitude (MSA: Minimum Safe Altitude in the U.S.)

Lowest safe altitude for a given air route with a safety margin over the highest obstacle. Allows for the aircraft straying say 2,000 ft off-course. Over congested areas clearance must be 1,000 ft, while for populated areas it might be 500 ft. Over open water or sparsely populated areas, it might be less but require a minimum horizontal distance of at least 500 ft from any person, vessel, vehicle, or structure.

MANPADS: Man-Portable Air Defense Systems
Shoulder-launched antiaircraft missiles such as the ones used to attack the DHL Airbus taking off from Baghdad Airport.

Mach
Mach is the ratio of an aircraft's airspeed to the speed-of-sound in the ambient air around it.

Thus, an aircraft flying at Mach 1 is flying at the speed of sound, and one flying at Mach 2 is flying at twice the speed of sound.

An interesting point is that the speed of sound varies with temperature (not pressure), with Mach 1 being about 15% less in terms of airspeed at a cruising height of some 35,000ft where it is very cold.

Typical cruise speed for the Boeing 747 at 35000 feet

- Mach 0.855 = 567 MPH (912 km/h).

Airliners have Mach Indicators enabling the pilots and autopilot to determine the Mach speed without calculating it according to the external temperature.

See Subsonic and Supersonic.

Maximum Permissible Takeoff Weight
The maximum permissible take-off weight of an aircraft depends on a number of factors, including the wind speed/direction, the temperature and altitude of the airport (the hotter and higher the airport, the more difficult it is for the aircraft to take off).

The overall weight of the aircraft [See AUW/All Up Weight] increases according to the amount of fuel carried, and the combined weight of freight (including baggage) and passengers.

Apart from the maximum permissible takeoff weight determined according to the above conditions, there is another limiting factor, which might come into play in the case of very powerful engines able to get the aircraft into the air regardless of the conditions. That is the limit imposed by the structural strength of the aircraft. This was mentioned in the case of the fatal supersonic Concorde flight from Paris, where the aircraft was on paper close to its structural takeoff weight limit, and probably well over it as certain items of baggage were not taken into account and even the actual average weight of the passengers must have been quite high. See Maximum Zero Fuel Weight below.

Maximum Zero Fuel Weight
Airliners carry fuel in central fuel tanks in the fuselage and perhaps most importantly of all in the wings. The advantage of having fuel in the wings is that the wings lift the fuel at the same time as they lift the aircraft and strengthened wing mountings to support are not needed.

It sometimes happens that a long-range aircraft designed to carry a great load of fuel in the wings is assigned to a short leg with hardly any fuel but with a lot of heavy freight in addition to a full load of passengers. Since this would all be concentrated in the fuselage, it could mean that although the All Up Weight is well within the limits, the bending moment at the wing roots would be excessive. To guard against this, airliners also have a *maximum zero fuel weight*.

MAYDAY ... MAYDAY ... MAYDAY

Prefix to distress call, equivalent to SOS in Morse code days. Derived from the French, *M'aidez!*, meaning *Help Me!*

When an emergency arises, pilots change their Transponder Squawk Code to the Emergency Code, which is 7700 in the U.S. If they are very busy dealing with the emergency, they may not have time to issue a MAYDAY call immediately, and only reset the Transponder. In the case of the Air France Airbus A330 lost between Brazil and France, they did not even have time to do that.

Much less known, is the quasi-distress call PAN ... PAN ... PAN, transmitted in the case of the fatal Swissair flight from New York's Kennedy Airport when the pilots smelt smoke but initially did not think situation too serious.

MD (McDonnell Douglas)

Bought by Boeing in 1997

MD-80 Series [1980] 800+

This second-generation DC-9 medium size medium range airliner has been very successful and many still operating.

MD-90 [1995] 114

A stretched version of the MD-80 with other enhancements, but less successful, in part because production ceased in 2000 because no further orders taken following purchase of McDonnell Douglas by Boeing in 1997—it would have competed with other Boeing aircraft, notably the 737.

MEL: Minimum Equipment List

With thousands of items of equipment featuring in the modern airliner there will virtually always be something that is not working, be it an instrument with a failed light bulb or something major. Essential equipment is often in triplicate, but that is often so important that no aircraft would take off with one of the three not working.

When an aircraft enters service, the manufacturer supplies a Minimum Equipment List (MEL) and as experience is gained, the manufacturer and airline update this. The MEL specifies what must be working for the flight to be allowed to take off. Sometimes, special precautions and conditions are attached. An extreme case might be the ferrying of a 4-engine BA 747 back to London from Tokyo on three engines for servicing subject to there being specially trained pilots and no passengers.

A famous misapplication of the MEL was the *Gimli Glider* case where an airliner ran out of fuel over Canada in consequence and thanks to the captain's experience on gliders was able to land hard but safely at a small airfield called Gimli. See *Air Crashes and Miracle Landings*.

METAR: aviation routine weather report

Standardized weather report issued hourly (except in the case of radical changes) by airfields and permanent meteorological stations.

Pilots and aircraft dispatchers use METARs for flight planning, and *en route* updates. Said to be derived from the French MÉTéorologique Aviation Régulière.

METARS reports are generated automatically, whereas a human produces TAFs (Terminal Aerodrome/Area Forecasts) though not necessarily by someone actually stationed at the site in question.

Microsoft Flight Simulator™

Using this program with a reasonable PC one can learn to fly around the world in anything from small GA aircraft to the largest airliners.

Unfortunately, Microsoft is no longer supporting the program itself, perhaps because so many copies were pirated.

Military Contribution to Civilian Airliner Programs

U.S. companies and Boeing in particular, complain about Airbus receiving what they call unfair subsidies in the form of soft loans on non-commercial terms. The European counter-argument is that Boeing's profitable military contracts represent an equivalent or even greater subsidy.

In truth, the advantage that Boeing has accrued from its military work may be more subtle, and greater than apparent:

- The prototype for the Boeing 707, the Boeing 367-80 referred to as the Dash-Eighty, was developed largely in the expectation of orders for what was to become the K-135 tanker.

- The Boeing 747—with its abnormally high flight deck—was the offspring of a cancelled project undertaken in the hope of orders for a large military transport able to be loaded from the front under the pilots.

It was not all military gravy as subsequent development of these highly successful airliners involved virtually betting the company in view of the financial risk. However, without the military component, would there have been a 707 or indeed a 747?

Missed Approach

When an aircraft is making a landing under IFR (Instrument Flight Rules) the pilots may decide, or very often be ordered, to abandon the landing for any number of reasons, including

- Being unable to see the runway when down to the decision height.
- Being badly lined-up, or too high.
- Aircraft not properly stabilized, or traveling too fast.
- Windshear, or crosswind exceeding company limits.
- Presence of another aircraft on the runway.

If that is the case, the pilot then initiates the go-around and missed approach procedure, which the pilots always have in their mind or Flight Director as they come in. That in particular includes the prescribed missed approach exit route for the runway in question, ensuring that they avoid collision with other aircraft or obstacles, and the instructions about where to hold before making another landing attempt—conditions permitting

While experience has shown diverting to an alternate (airport) to be often the best course, there can be great pressure on a captain not to do so. There is cost to the airline of a diversion involving the booking of hotel rooms and the aircraft being out of position for the next flight, not to mention the pilot's personal plans. While no sensible captain will allow these factors to be decisive, there can be grey areas where such factors could tip the balance.

A case where a diversion would have been a better option was the Thai Airlines crash at Surat Thani where the pilot made two missed approaches in bad weather and crashed on the third, even though company regulations stipulated a diversion after two failed attempts. Some commentators have suggested that VIPs on board pressured him to land.

There was also the Air France overrun in bad weather at Montreal, where the aircraft ended up in a gully and caught fire with all passengers evacuating safely despite many carrying their hand luggage.

Mode

Webopedia aptly defines mode as *the state or setting of a program or device.*

A number of the devices displays and computers in airliner cockpits can be set to act in different modes (or ways) according to what the pilots intend to do. Failure to understand the implications of a mode or even selecting the wrong mode by mistake has led to catastrophic accidents. The Mont Saint Odile Airbus crash in France was possibly a typical case.

MORA: Minimum Off-Route Altitude

Most Dangerous Phases of a Flight

Taking off and landing are potentially the most dangerous phases of the flight.

- Taking off is dangerous because the aircraft is heavy with flammable fuel and does not have so much safety margin regarding speed and height if something goes wrong. However, when taking off, the pilots at least usually know where the ground, runway and nearby high obstacles are, which is not always true when landing!

- Landing is potentially dangerous when weather conditions are bad, but not necessarily so if pilots are prepared to divert if at all doubtful.

MRCC: Maritime Rescue Coordination Center

MRO: Maintenance, Repair and Overhaul

This is a key aspect of safe and efficient airline operations, and one where IT (Information Technology) and Data Mining are playing an increasing role. See SMS.

MSA: Minimum Safe Altitude

Altitude in a given area below which aircraft under IFR are not allowed to go without specific permission from ATC.

MTOW: Maximum TakeOff Weight

See Maximum Takeoff Weight.

Mules (a warning!)

Passengers transporting drugs etc. for dealers, often by swallowing pellets or more usually condoms packed with them. The latter sometimes split with fatal results. Mules may give themselves away by refusing onboard refreshments and catering.

Countries in South-East Asia such as Thailand, Singapore and Malaysia, where trafficking significant amounts of drugs can incur the death penalty, often treat mules very harshly. It is no consolation to parents to learn that their offspring staying at the *"Bangkok Hilton"*—ironical nickname for the local prison and the subject of novels—were probably denounced to the authorities by the very people who conned them into accepting the drugs in the first place.

Most mules know what they are doing without realizing the risks and implications. However, taking something on an aircraft without knowing or not knowing what it is can be even more dangerous. In one case, in the course of routine pre-flight questioning of a young pregnant woman about to travel on an El Al flight, Israeli security people learnt she was not the only person involved in the packing and discovered her nice "boyfriend" had placed a bomb in her suitcase.

N1 & N2

Turbofan jet engines at present have at least two spools:

- Spool 1 consists of the so-called front fan hard-mounted on a center shaft going right through to turbines hard mounted on it at the rear,

- and Spool 2 in the middle with a hollow shaft mounted coaxially on the first shaft so that the two rotate independently of each other.

The respective rotational speeds, N_1 and N_2, of the two indicate the amount of thrust and the performance. Unlike the rev counters in an automobile, N_1 & N_2 express the rate of rotation as a percentage of their rated or maximum normal speed. To maximize engine life, pilots try to keep significantly below 100%. However, in an emergency they might even go above 100%! See EPR.

[Unless the gears break, the ratio between N1 and N2 would obviously be constant in the case of the new Geared Turbofan engines!]

Nacelles

In jet aircraft, the nacelles are the engine inlets and housing, including the thrust reverser cowling and outlet. Although seemingly unremarkable, their conception is a critical factor in how the engines perform and the aircraft flies.

Nanosatellite (Micro-satellite)

Rather confusing term used by NASA and the military for micro-satellites.

These are somewhat like footballs, say 20 cm in diameter, and weigh some 5kg. They can be deployed from spacecraft to make inspections with cameras.

The term is confusing term because nanotechnology is not a key feature if featuring at all—at least for the moment.

Narrow-Body

Traditionally airliners had a single aisle with two or three seats on either side. This could be achieved with a fuselage (tube) diameter of up to a maximum of about 4 meters (12ft). The thinking was that a larger diameter tube would increase drag and hence fuel consumption. However, with airlines wanting to carry more passengers per aircraft and more space, commercial and other advantages of a *wide-body* design became apparent for some applications. See Wide-body.

NASA: National Air & Space Administration

Photos and videos of astronauts landing on the moon and space shuttle launches, not to mention other publicity, give the impression that NASA is primarily concerned with astronautics.

In fact, the contribution NASA is making in the aviation domain is considerable. This is particularly true of NASA's Dryden facility.

National Air & Space Museum (Washington): NASM

The most visited museum in the United States, with many younger visitors. Extensive collection of exhibits ranging from Wright Brothers' craft to actual space flight capsules. Entrance: Free.

The Annex to the museum (situated near Dulles International Airport) has a great collection of the larger aircraft. Coaches ply between the main museum and the Annex.

[Some readers might find it helpful to know, as in the case of the author, that the mid-market *Holiday Inn Capitol Hotel is* located very close to both the museum and the FAA, with the NTSB within walking distance.]

Nautical Mile: nm

One minute of arc of latitude on Earth's surface. See Coordinates.

16% longer than a Statute Mile at 1.16 m, or 1.853 km.

Used for aerial navigation as well as navigation on sea. Aircraft speeds are always in Knots (nm per hour).

Navaid

Radio navigation aid.

ND: Navigation Display

NDB: Non-Directional Beacon

Navigational beacons broadcasting on medium frequencies whose bearing can be detected using the aircraft's ADF (Automatic Direction Finder). The use of medium radio frequencies instead of VHF makes them visible over the horizon and therefore valuable for low-flying aircraft. See ADF.

Near Miss

A near miss is defined as aircraft coming within certain distance. Very often signifies the aircraft were closer than they should have been, but not really in danger of colliding. U.K. Ministry of Defense defines it as cases where pilots think they were dangerously close.

NextGen: Next Generation Air Traffic Control System

FAA's program to revolutionize every aspect of the United States ATC system which in many ways is quite antiquated and unsuited to the increasing demands likely to be placed on it.

The FAA has to continue to finance and upgrade present equipment while investing in the system for the future.

At the heart of NextGen is ADS-B, where traditional radar is complemented by a system whereby aircraft continually broadcast their position determined by onboard GPS. See ADS-B.

The comprehensive list of NextGen acronyms published by the FAA is a good gateway to the subject:

http://www.faa.gov/about/office_org/headquarters_offices/ato/publications/ nextgenplan/0608/acronyms/

Nine-Eleven (9/11)

Short-hand in the U.S. for the events of September 11, 2001, where 4 aircraft were hijacked, with 2 flown into the World Trade Center in New York, 1 flown into the Pentagon in Washington, and one crashing before reaching its target, which possibly had been the Capitol building in Washington. Term gained currency because multiple targets involved. In the U.S., dates are written with the month (September) first.

Nm: nautical miles

1.16 Statute Miles or 1.853 km.

Number 1, 2, or 3 engine?

An aircraft's engines are numbered from left to right, looking forwards.

On a twinjet, the No. 2 engine would be the right-hand one; on a trijet with one engine at the rear, the No. 2 engine would be the one in the middle but at the rear.

Non-Stop Flights

Recently the improved performance and range of aircraft has resulted in a rush by airlines to provide non-stop flights to long-haul destinations with some even involving flight times of as long as 18 hours, with 12-hour flights, such as from London to Tokyo or Hong Kong, being commonplace.

These are very popular with passengers as they shorten journey times by at least two hours, and have made more direct routing possible. What the airlines lost in fuel efficiency—fuel has to be used to transport fuel for the latter part of the journey that could have been put on board mid-way—they made up in other ways. These include not having to pay landing charges and staff at stopover points; poaching passengers from competitors or rather not losing them; in the case of business passengers being able to charge a premium; and less disruption to schedules due to unexpected delays at en route stops.

However, if fuel becomes much more expensive the total cost could outweigh the above advantages. With the surge in fuel price in 2008, some of the ultra-long haul non-stops, such Thai Airways Bangkok to New York and Bangkok to Los Angeles flights which took about 17 hours to fly the approximately 13,000 km (8647 mile) routes were discontinued.

Thai Airways estimated that continuing the non-stop New York and Los Angeles routes would cause it to lose 120 million dollars a year. According to Thai Airways' Mr. Pandit (quoted by the *Bangkok Post*):

> *Fuel on THAI's Bangkok-New York flight makes up 55% of its operating costs, exceeding the 34% average.*

> *When the ultra long-haul flights to New York were taking shape on THAI's drawing board in 2003, jet fuel was 82 U.S. cent per gallon, but since then they have zoomed to $1.62 in 2005 when the flights began. Fuel surged to $2.20 in 2007 before skyrocketing to more than $4.00—killing the economics of the service.*

Singapore Airlines was faced with the same fuel penalty problem on its ultra-long haul flights on very similar routes, but was been able to soften the blow by having an all-business class service, something that Thai could not do with Bangkok not being a financial/business hub. However, with financial institutions reducing staff and spending, Singapore Airlines cannot be viewing the situation with total equanimity.

Many people mistakenly believe that the term *Direct Flight* so often used by travel agents means a Non-Stop Flight, when it only means the flight is effected in the same aircraft or, worse still, merely with different aircraft given the same the same flight number.

Normal Accident

In a famous book entitled *Normal Accidents—Living with High Risk Technologies*, the organizational analyst and sociologist, Professor Charles Perrow, has coined the apparently contradictory term *normal accident*. He exhaustively studied many of the recent super-accidents, such as Bhopal (Chemicals), Three Mile Island (Nuclear), Chernobyl (Nuclear), and a ferry accident in the North Sea. He concluded that accidents are inevitable in complex systems, and that sometimes it is the systems installed to promote safety that become the cause, with linkage between different subsystems, leading to cascading linked events resulting in disaster. On the other hand, he has argued that despite these negative aspects, on balance, the impact of these new technologies, such as nuclear power, is positive since achieving the same goal by other means would be even more risky in terms of human lives.

Northrop-Grumman

In terms of revenue from defense (See Defense News), Northrop-Grumman is the fourth largest defense contractor with 78% of its revenue deriving from defense. Interestingly, the way they use the word systems to define their wide range of activities in the aerospace domain is a lesson in new terminology. Rather than mentioning the name of the actual products, such as fighters, bombers and so on, they classify them, logically enough, as systems. They have, strategic systems, theater systems, and so on.

Areas of activity are

- Information and Services
- Electronics
- Aerospace—extensive, but their last large manned a/c program was the B-2 Spirit stealth bomber in the 1990s.
- Shipbuilding
- Expertise in one area is applicable in the other areas and one cannot but see some parallels as regards terminology strategies with France's Thales, except that Thales does not build actual aircraft of any size.

Northrop-Grumman *thought* it had won an enormous contract to be the final integrator in collaboration with EADS/Airbus for a refueling tanker for the U.S. Air Force based on the Airbus A330. Partly due to questions raised concerning the tendering process and partly because of political pressure in favor of Boeing and a domestic solution, the decision was overturned and put off until later.

NOTAM: Notice to Airmen
These are official warnings and updates regarding situations and notably potential hazards at airports and en route. Typical information would be runways/taxiways closed for repairs, faulty runway lighting, presence of birds, and temporarily restricted airspace due to flights by heads of state, air shows and parachute drops, airspace closed for military activity, and inoperable navigation aids.

NTSB: National Transportation Safety Board
Although the NTSB figures prominently in air crash investigations, one should not forget its remit covers all modes of transport. Notably, its work recently included issuing warnings about the possible use of cell phone texting prior to a railroad crash and cases of teenagers texting before automobile crashes.

In the aviation sphere, the NTSB is viewed as the noble guy, while the FAA has to steer a difficult course between various interests. The NTSB can recommend, but it is the FAA that has to implement those recommendations or otherwise.

The NTSB is respected worldwide for its investigative expertise.

It has a list of MOST WANTED measures that the FAA should take:

- Improve Safety of Emergency Medical Services Flights
  - Conduct all flights with medical personnel on board in accordance with commuter aircraft (regulations) ...

- Improve Runway Safety
  - Give immediate warnings of probable collisions/incursions directly to cockpit flight crews.
  - Require specific air traffic control clearance for each runway crossing.
  - Install cockpit moving map displays or automatic systems to alert pilots of attempted takeoffs from taxiways or wrong runways.
  - Require landing distance assessment with an adequate safety margin.
  - Reduce Dangers to Aircraft Flying in Icing Conditions
  - Use current research on freezing rain and large water droplets to revise the way aircraft are designed and approved for flight in icing conditions.
  - Apply revised icing requirements to currently certificated aircraft.
  - Require that airplanes with pneumatic deice boots activate boots as soon as the airplane enters icing conditions.
- Improve Crew Resource Management
  - Require commuter and on-demand air taxi flight crews to receive crew resource management training.
- Require Image Recorders
  - Install crash-protected image recorders in cockpits to give investigators more information to solve complex accidents.
- Reduce Accidents and Incidents Caused by Human Fatigue
  - Set working hour limits for flight crews, aviation mechanics and air traffic controllers based on fatigue research, circadian rhythms, and sleep and rest requirements.
  - Develop a fatigue awareness and countermeasures program for air traffic controllers.

The NTSB updates the list from time to time.
See http://ntsb.gov/recs/mostwanted/aviation_issues.htm

Onboard Threat Detection System

One of the Paris-based *Security Of Aircraft In The Future European Environment* (SAFEE) research projects, whereby a camera and microphone in the seatback in front of a passenger would measure blink rates and facial twitches to determine stress levels and listen out for phrases such as Allah Akbar indicating the presence of terrorists about to go into action. Chemical sniffers could be included and passengers deemed somewhat suspicious could be made to sit in high surveillance zones.

Objections on privacy grounds are countered by saying the data would be deleted at the end of the flight. Could be a means of listening-in to conversations for business advantage, but at least passengers would be aware of this. Some years ago, U.S. officials were warning high-level officials and CEOs travelling First Class on a certain European airline about microphones embedded in the seats by the country's secret service.

Octas

Amount of cloud cover is expressed in octas (eighths).

Cloud of *6 octas* means six-eighths of the sky is covered by cloud. The height of the cloud and sometimes type are likely to be specified too.

Oil Crises of 1974 and 1979

When the Anglo-French supersonic Concorde was being offered to airlines before the oil crises of 1974 and 1979, jet fuel cost 11 cents per gallon, and even though airline executives thought this situation would continues, U.S. airlines declined to buy it. By 1980, the price was $1 a gallon.

This increase in price encouraged airlines to seek more fuel-efficient airliners, just as is the case now following the more recent oil shocks.

Open jaw (ticket)

An open jaw ticket is a ticket where there is a break in the series of stopping off points. In simplest form, it could mean flying say from London to Washington DC and flying back to London from New York, with the leg between the two cities accomplished by another means, such as the train or even another carrier.

Open Skies Agreement

As mentioned under the Freedoms entry, the negotiation of flying rights between governments can be a cutthroat business. At one time, a country's airline was often its flag carrier and government-owned, with that government doing everything possible to protect it. Such airlines still benefit from bilateral agreements. British Airways benefits from bilateral agreements in additional to having guaranteed traffic thanks to its possession of so many Slots at the world's busiest international airport, London's Heathrow.

Bilateral agreements pertained all through the world, but those with the U.S., and particularly between the U.S. and Europe, being especially important in view of the amount of traffic and the then ability of passengers on those routes to pay high fares. Notable agreements were the Bermuda Agreements, named after the island where the first Bermuda Agreement was made in 1946. A key feature of these agreements was the designation of two carriers from each country with the main rights to fly between the main airports.

With the worldwide move towards more freedom many restrictions have been reduced with the U.S. pushing its own version of Open Skies, which to some does not appear so open in that it restricts Cabotage in the U.S. In addition, the Fly America obligation, whereby federal employees and subcontractors are obliged to use U.S. airlines is deemed restrictive.

Anyway, the U.S. recently signed an Open Skies Agreement with the European Union, which according to the E.U. supersedes any such U.K. agreement.

Outer marker

Point indicated by a *marker* where descent to the runway using instruments usually begins. Marker often takes the form of a vertically emitting radio beacon that will produce an indication in the cockpit as the aircraft passes over it.

Overrun

An overrun really means being unable to stop before reaching the end of the paved runway, either when landing, or after aborting a takeoff. It is sometimes referred to as *overshooting*.

As technology has improved and reduced the incidence of other types of accident, such as Controlled Flight into Terrain (CFIT), runway overruns, especially on landing in bad weather, are coming to the forefront as the cause of major accidents. There have been a number of cases, such as the Qantas 100-M.P.H. overrun at Bangkok and the Air France overrun at Montreal, which could have resulted in great loss of life. In addition, there were others where there was loss of life.

Overspeed

Each aircraft type has airspeed limits for various configurations ranging from Clean Configuration to maximum flap and undercarriage lowered. Should the airspeed exceed these limits the instruments give an *overspeed* warning. Exceeding the limits by a significant amount or for a lengthy period could result in damage to the aircraft or even it breaking up.

Pairing

Just as airlines avoid rostering two pilots who have little experience on a given aircraft type together, they also try to avoid having two extremely old pilots flying together. See Age of Pilot.

Pan Am (Pan American World Airways)

There was a time when Americans traveling abroad would proudly say they had come on Pan Am; now the younger ones hardly know the name of what was once America's *de facto* flag carrier. It now no longer exists.

One of Pan Am's weaknesses was the lack of a domestic network. Airlines like British Overseas Airways (BOAC) had some things in common with Pan Am, but the British government defended their carrier's interests and even when the situation became more competitive, the airline's possession of so many of the prized Slots at London's Heathrow meant the airline could always make money. BOAC subsequently merged with British European Airways (BEA) to form British Airways.

After a Pan Am 747 was brought blown up by a bomb placed in luggage over Lockerbie in Scotland, some people hesitated to fly with the airline fearing its fame would always make it a prime target for terrorists.

Juan Trippe, the airline's founder and dominating figure over many years, played a major role in the introduction of the Boeing 707 and 747. See Juan Trippe.

PAN ... PAN ... PAN!

See MAYDAY.

Passports (biometric)

With passports being stolen, forged and altered on the one hand and the fear of terrorist action rising following Nine-Eleven, there have been general moves to introduce biometric passports incorporating electronic chips giving physical and other information.

Patrick Smith

Commercial pilot (amongst other things), Patrick Smith has a witty aviation blog on the U.S. website salon.com with comments and info on the latest happenings, be they crashes or the over-the-top actions of TSA staff.

Also has a useful book, *Ask The Pilot*, based on those pieces and aimed at the general public.

PCA: Propulsion Controlled Aircraft

Maneuvering an an aircraft using engine power alone in case of total failure of hydraulics—no rudder, no ailerons, no elevators, etc.

Idea is to use computer software rather than humans to achieve this. NASA's Dryden Flight Research Center did work on this some years but abandoned it for cost-benefit reasons. Interest has been rekindled due to the increasing terrorist threat from shoulder-launched missiles.

As an interim measure in the U.S.A, it has been decided to give pilots some instruction on how to handle an aircraft manually in such circumstances, as control inputs required are far from obvious. See Phugoid.

PCAR: Propulsion Controlled Aircraft Recovery
Name given by U.S. Department of Home Security (DHS) to reactivated program started at Dryden to control crippled airliners. See PCA above.

Pentagon
Term used to denote the decisions made at the top of the U.S. military and the vast 5-sided (pentagon-shaped) 5-storey building complex housing the Department of Defense in Virginia State. While situated in Virginia adjacent to Washington D.C., it has special Washington DC postcodes (ZIP codes) for its mail.

The Pentagon was built in only 16 months following the groundbreaking ceremony in September 1941, as there was a pressing need to bring together the various branches of the military scattered around the capital in World War II.

It owes its shape to the fact that the U.S. Congress originally granted approval for a design configured for a plot bounded by five roads. Following objections that placing the building on that plot would block the wonderful view of the Capitol that one had from the tomb of Pierre L'Enfant, the French architect-engineer who planned Washington, in Arlington National Cemetery a second site on nearby land with the same designation was chosen. Keeping the original overall design avoided the need for lengthy re-approval from Congress. In fact, freedom from geographical constraints of the original roads meant it was possible to construct a regular pentagon.

Perrow, Professor Charles B.
See Normal Accident.

PF: Pilot Flying
The pilot actually handling the aircraft, it being made clear between them who has that responsibility, with the pilot taking over saying: *'I have control'*. Usually, pilots take turns—on short flights, one pilot might fly the outward leg and the other the return leg. In an emergency, or extremely difficult weather conditions the captain would normally take over, provided enough time remains for him or her to get the *feel* of the aircraft in time. The PNF (Pilot Not Flying) is usually busy too, handling radio communications with ATC, etc.

PFD: Primary Flight Display
In modern airliners and increasingly in business jets, the mechanical gauges, and sometimes-confusing LED gauges, have been relegated to serving as backups with their information displayed on a LCD or CRT device in a Primary Flight Display in the so-called *glass cockpit*. This makes it much easier for pilots to see at a glance what is happening, as they do not have to scan the gauges and indicators individually. The PFD will show everything the pilot traditionally needs to know to determine his or her situation

- simulated artificial horizon

- airspeed
- altitude
- vertical speed (climb rate or importantly sink rate)

Furthermore, presets on the Flight Director/Autopilot are flagged by Bugs on the altitude and airspeed scales indicating to pilots how close they are to the desired value and reminded them what that value was. See Glass Cockpit.

PFR: Post Flight Report

Phugoid

Inherent *porpoise* like motion of an aircraft evident in the absence of functioning elevators to halt it. The nose pitches up, and then, as the speed consequently decreases, the nose pitches down. Then the same happens in vice-versa with that pitching down of the nose making the speed increase and the nose pitch up, and so on and so on. In large aircraft, the oscillatory period can be several minutes. Difficult to control by engine power alone as when the aircraft speeds up and slows the pilot is liable to reduce or add power just when doing so will only accentuate the phugoid motion. See *Uncontrollable JAL 747* in main book and Counter Intuitivity.

PIREP: Pilot's Reports

Reports by pilots regarding weather conditions encountered en route and even on landing (braking) retransmitted by land stations in standard format for the benefit of other aircraft. They normally have the prefix UA, but this is changed to UUA when hazardous conditions are involved.

Piggybacking

Manufacturers using approvals and certifications obtained for earlier models or similar models of an aircraft to get approval for derivatives, thus avoiding the cost of retesting or new trials. The Boeing 737 and future 747-8 being examples. Similar to Grandfathering.

Pilot Training (becoming a pilot)

Traditionally in the U.S. and in other countries, a pilot not trained by the military would have gone to flying school, become an instructor, and then AFTER gaining considerable experience have got a job at an airline.

While the FAA favors this system, a recent issue of the U.K.'s *Flight International* quotes a number of aviation training experts at U.S. universities and flying schools, as saying

> *Such training prepares you for flying an aircraft by yourself, while at an airline you don't really fly anything by yourself.*

Another expert argues that resources should not be spent on students who do not have *what it takes*, saying

> *Now the only qualification to train as a pilot is (having) a MasterCard,*

adding that the free market is the wrong selection process—an argument that would apply to doctors in many countries.

In view of the shortage of pilots in the U.S., partly because of demands from China and India, changes will come about. Other countries have various schemes not dependent on MasterCards. Interestingly, an airline in China is for the first time allowing some students to pay for training in Australia.

Pitot tube (Pitot Probe)

Based on a 300-year old idea of French Professor Pitot, the pitot tube is in its simplest form is a forwards-facing hollow probe with a hole at its tip into which the oncoming air (referred to as *ram air*) rushes and a sideways facing hole measuring the static pressure independently of the speed of the aircraft. By comparing the two, the airspeed can be computed. In that form, it is referred to as a pitot-static tube.

In the case of the modern airliner, that set-up is more complicated with the static ports not necessarily on the pitot probe, and there always being three sets so that the one that fails can be identified as the odd man out.

This strategy would not work should two fail, say due to the buildup of ice crystals. Nozzles are fitted with heaters to prevent them icing up, but even so, there have been problems.

See: *757 Blindfolded by Forgotten Masking Tape (Lima, 1996)* in *Air Crashes and Miracle Landings.*

Pitot-Static System

System consisting of pitot tubes, static ports, connecting tubes, pressure sensors and instruments used to determine, airspeed, altitude, and rate of climb and descent (sink rate).

Planetary Gears/Cyclic gears

Extremely rugged and compact gearing system having a *sun* gear in the middle meshing with often 3 or 5 *planet* gears around it which in turn mesh with a ring (annulus) embracing them all. Used in many applications but most notably as regards aviation in the Pratt and Whitney Geared Turbofan engine which is expected to be more fuel efficient as the gearing will enable the fan and turbines to operate at optimum speeds.

PNF: Pilot Not Flying

See PF.

Pods (engines mounted in pods under wings)

Airliners used to have their engines set in the wings. Then there seemed to be a fashion to have them at the tail, giving a cleaner wing much favored by Russian designers. Now engines are mostly placed in pods under the wings.

This has a number of advantages including

- Easier servicing
- Wider choice of engines, as only the pylons have to be changed
- Easier recovery from a stall, although application of sudden power at low airspeeds can push the nose up dangerously if the engines are very low slung
- Engines can be placed far out on the wing which itself shields some of the noise, thus reducing cabin noise
- As explained in the Maximum Zero Fuel Weight entry, since the wings do the lifting there are structural advantages in their lifting the (heavy) engines at the same time
- Engine pylons can be designed to allow engines to drop off in the event of a catastrophic failure or on ditching or on encountering an obstacle.

Disadvantages:

- Does not allow such a clean aerodynamic design thus incurring penalties as regards drag;
- Low-slung engines pick up more extraneous matter, as was the case with the 737 at some sandy/dusty unpaved airports;
- Engines slung under the wings are liable to snag and cause the aircraft to cartwheel or worse when ditching in water. In theory this should not happen if coming down with wings level as the pylons are designed to break off when pod subjected to extreme backwards force when striking an object (pylons need to be resistant to forward forces as that is the way the engines are pushing the aircraft forwards).

Pond: Atlantic Ocean

The phrase *across the pond* may mean across the Atlantic. Often suggests the speaker is so important that the Atlantic is no big thing and that he or she functions on both sides. Use by people in aviation perhaps more justified than by others.

Pork Barrel

Derogatory term in the U.S. for defense, agricultural and infrastructure projects and the like paid for by taxpayers as a whole but benefitting the electors of the particular Congressional member supporting the legislation allocating the funds. Airbus counter Boeing's objections to the governmental loans it receives by saying that Boeing benefits from pork barrel military contracts and funds received for research, not to mention the skewing of military procurement decisions as in the case of airborne refueling tanker.

PPL: Private Pilots License

License (Certificate) allowing an individual to pilot certain aircraft not for hire. Requires a minimum of 40 or 45 hours flight (training) experience and written and practical tests.

Preflight Inspection (Walk Around)

An often somewhat cursory external inspection of the aircraft by the copilot or other junior member of the aircrew prior to every flight.

The check is performed in addition to those much more extensive checks made by mechanics. Could be compared with the motorist (ideally) checking for obvious faults before setting off. Health and safety rules allegedly prevent the officer climbing up into wheel bays, where stowaways facing almost certain death might be hiding.

Pressurization (of cabin)

Cabins are usually maintained at a pressure equivalent to 8,000ft.

See Depressurization.

PPRuNe: Professional Pilots Rumour Network

'An aviation website dedicated to airline pilots and those who are considering a career as a commercial Aviation'.

www.pprune.org/

QC: Quota Count

Term used in a quota system to encourage the use of quieter aircraft.

Aircraft types are given a Quota Count (QC) value, according to how much noise they make on landing and take-off.

These are QC0.25, QC0.5, QC1, QC2, QC4, QC8 and QC16 (the noisiest category).

Aircraft movements score QC values against a maximum allowable Quota for each season. At London's Gatwick, this might be 6,700 for summer and 2,300 for winter between 11:30pm and 6am (the night quota period).

An aircraft manufacturer such as Boeing will for instance try and claim that one of its aircraft does better in this regard compared with the equivalent made by its competitor.

Q-codes (QFE & QNR)

Remnants of codes left over from wireless-telegraphy days, where a 3-letter code would be used to represent a frequently used phrase or sentence.

Perhaps the best-known Q-code outside aviation is QRM in radio communication where it means wireless interference.

In aviation, there is QDM to indicate the magnetic bearing to a station, and the well-known ones used inform pilots of the adjustments that have to be made to the atmospheric altimeter subscale to give the height above the airfield in question or above sea level:

- QFE simply being the atmospheric pressure at that airfield and in theory, an aircraft on the ground there should have it altimeter showing roughly zero with this setting.

- QNE being the mean sea level pressure estimated from that at the airfield or ATC facility and should mean the altimeter will indicate the height of the aircraft above mean sea level in that vicinity.

Quick Access Data Recorder (QADR)
Data recorder that can be accessed quickly and easily by maintenance staff to obtain data of value for servicing—even revealing such details as tire pressures. Unlike the Flight Data Recorder, it is not designed to withstand extreme heat, shock and great depths of water. Mentioned in connection with the 100-M.P.H. Qantas overrun at Bangkok.

Radar: Radio Detection and Ranging
A similar system to that used by bats, but using radio waves instead of sound waves, to detect objects and determine their distance.

The British did much of the initial development work on radar, referring to it as RDF (Radio Direction Finding). The term *radar (Radio Detection and Ranging)* was proposed by Commander S. M. Tucker of the U.S. Navy in 1940, and was soon adopted in the U.S. It was not until 1943 that it officially replaced the term RDF in the U.K.

Many very capable scientists worked on radar projects during WWII, with those conceiving devices able to produce high power at very short wavelengths featuring prominently in the latter part of the war.

Military radar depended on the detection of radio waves bounced back from the surface of an aircraft. When used after the war for civilian air traffic control, controllers would normally have to order an aircraft to make a turn in order to make a positive identification. Another problem was that the weakened signal bounced back from a single aircraft could easily get lost amongst the clutter also on the monitor.

It was then that another idea developed during the war, namely the IFF (Identification of Friend or Foe) device, came into play. The IFF device was simply a transponder that on receiving the radar pulse replied that the aircraft was friendly.

Adapting the principle for use in Air Traffic Control, the transponder now not only indicates the identity (Flight Number), but also the height of the aircraft and whether the situation is normal or an emergency.

Furthermore, the signal squawked back is many times stronger than one merely bounced off the surface of the aircraft. See Squawk.

Primary Radar

- Radar based on the old military principle of bouncing back the signal transmitted.

Secondary Radar

- Radar depending on use of a transponder to send back an echo with data about identity, altitude and status (say emergency).

  N.B. Secondary radar used by ATC, merely indicates the altitude based on the same data used by the aircraft's altimeter so it is no good a pilot asking ATC to confirm his or her height other than in the event of their being blinded by smoke.

In one disaster involving a Peruvian airliner, an aircraft polisher left protective tape on the pitot and static tube inlets. Finally, over the sea at night with nothing visible, the pilots asked ATC for their altitude. Told they were at 9,700 ft as also shown by their altimeter, they hit the sea with the loss of all on board. Possibly, the information overload due to the spurious warnings from the data-starved computers prevented them thinking clearly, but they should have known not to rely on the height given by ATC, and have taken note of their radio altimeter.

Radar is now used in all sorts of domains ranging from finding dead bodies hidden in walls and under floors to detecting intercontinental missiles.

Radar has one military drawback, namely that switching it on makes the interrogator/seeker visible to the enemy.

Although we are all familiar with the rotating radar antennae at airports and on ships, these are mechanically vulnerable and slow. Now, the great progress in electronics and software is allowing their place to be taken in critical situations by phased array systems consisting of a number of fixed antennae triggered and scanned electronically to simulate rotating antennae. Patriot anti-missile systems and Aegis Class guided missile cruisers able to track 200 aircraft at a time, such as the U.S.S Vincennes that shot down the Iranian airliner, use phased arrays.

Radial

VOR radio beacons emit, amongst other things, two signals that when combined indicate the magnetic bearing in degrees of the aircraft from them, with each bearing quite sensibly being called a radial.

Radials are like the spokes of a bicycle wheel. An indicator in the cockpit shows whether the pilots are flying towards or from the beacon.

VOR beacons are used to indicate airways and pilots can be told to fly towards them after reaching a given radial (spoke). Just before the Tenerife disaster, air traffic control routinely gave the following ATC clearance

Proceed with heading 040 until intercepting the 325 radial from Las Palmas VOR.

Radio Altitude
Altitude given by radio altimeter—important when landing as certain automatic features and alerts depend upon it. However, can fluctuate disconcertingly say when the aircraft is passing over a clump of high trees.

Ranging
Term used to describe equipment that determines distance.

For example, there is the VOR (Very High Frequency Omni-directional Range beacon).

RAT (Ram Air Turbine)
An electric generator with windmill vanes attached deployed from the fuselage to generate emergency electrical power by wind milling should the engines stop functioning.

RDD: Radiological Dispersal Devices
Dirty bombs, which can be quite simple and small enough to be placed even in luggage.

Rearwards-Facing Seats
Just as baby seats in cars face backwards it seemingly would make sense to have passenger seats configured in the same way, and some military aircraft and business jets are so equipped—the U.K.'s RAF used to insist on it. Some business class cabins and business jets have some rearwards-facing seats, but not primarily for safety reasons.

See Seats for reasons cited for not having seats rearwards facing seats.

Also see Seat Belts.

Reason, Professor James
James Reason, Professor of Psychology at Manchester (England) University has done much to change the way safety is viewed not only in aviation, but also in many other industrial settings. He developed his model initially for the nuclear power industry. See Swiss Cheese Model.

Red-eye flight (Overnight flight)
Colloquial U.S. term for a flight departing between 9 p.m. and 5 a.m. Reporting of the O.J. Simpson trial made the term known outside the U.S.

Re-dispatch
Re-dispatching is where an airliner is Dispatched to one destination, and later, usually en route, re-dispatched to another.

Can be used an artifice to make non-stop long-haul flights where the aircraft is operating at its limit of endurance and cannot legally be dispatched to the intended destination because of insufficient fuel reserves. The aircraft is initially dispatched with a suitable airport say four-fifths of the way indicated as the destination. Then when on reaching there the pilots find—as will usually be the case—they have the required fuel reserves, they ask to be *re-dispatched* to their intended destination.

However, this demands acquiescence on the part of the authorities at the primary destination and subsequent destination, which may require their being under the same administration—as sometimes happens when the intermediate stop happens to be a mid-ocean island belonging to the country of destination.

The need to resort on occasions to this artifice can imply the aircraft is operating close to its limit, with the crew perhaps hesitating to take more circuitous routes to avoid storms or even taxi around the airport (using up fuel) in order to take off into a (light) headwind rather than having it as a tailwind. The German magazine *Der Spiegel* has suggested Air France flight AF447 lost between Rio de Janeiro and Paris was in such a situation and had the nearer Bordeaux as its flight plan destination on takeoff, and with little reserve of fuel was loathe to take a detour to avoid a storm.

The supersonic Concorde that crashed in Paris was also operating near it limit as regards fuel reserves and took off with a (light) tailwind. Admittedly, other factors, such as the delay incurred, would have influenced that decision.

Rejected Takeoff: RTO (Aborted Takeoff)
Pilots may abort a takeoff for many reasons, but will normally only do so before reaching the takeoff decision speed, V_1. After reaching V_1, the aircraft should be able to take off safely even should an engine fail.

If the takeoff is aborted when speed of the aircraft is approaching V_1, considerable braking generating much heat in the brakes may be required to arrest the aircraft, which in turn means a considerable time must be allowed for the brakes to cool before a new takeoff attempt is made.

Relight
A jet engine that has *flamed out* needs to be relit in order to supply power again. Sensors detect the extinction, and ignitors provide a powerful electric spark to relight it.

In the air, an engine can only be relit at certain airspeeds.

On the ground, an engine is often started using bleed air from the APU (Auxiliary Power Unit) to make it revolve, after which fuel is injected and ignited using the ignitors.

RFID: Radio Frequency IDentification
Tags, which are in effect mini-radio transponders, are increasingly being integrated into items—even the family pet—so that they can be identified by a reader in their proximity. Use being tried in aviation for identifying anything from aircraft parts to passengers' luggage.

Risk

The study of risk is a fascinating subject. This question is covered in *Air Crashes and Miracles Landings*, where the question as to whether it is safer to fly or to drive is considered—not as simple as it seems.

See Professors Perrow and Reason.

Rollover (helicopter)

Situation where one wheel or skid is snagged on an object or stuck to the ground, and the helicopter starts tipping and revolving around that point. A stage is reached at which no amount of control input can correct this and the craft keels over disastrously. The only solution is for the pilot to push the craft down onto the ground—something he or she might be loathe to do in a military confrontation or when trying to pluck someone from a place of incarceration.

Rollovers can also occur when the helicopter pilot is spatially disorientated in a Brownout. This can occur when the downwash from the rotors blows up a cloud of sand to produce almost zero visibility and with no points of visual reference. Rollovers occasioned by brownouts have been responsible for a number of helicopter losses in Iraq, though with the helicopters being near the ground they were not necessarily fatal for the occupants.

RMP: Radio Management Panel

ROT: Rate of Turn

GA aircraft flying relatively slowly usually have a turn indicator indicating a standard rate turn, which is 360 degrees in 2 minutes, and which is equivalent to 3 degrees per second.

Airliners do not really use standard rate turns as such, but use the maximum bank angle setting, with normally a limit of 30 degrees for manual flight and 25 degrees for the Flight Director. Thus, the rate of turn would depend on the bank angle setting and of course the airspeed.

Maximum bank angle would be 45 degrees except in emergencies, with 30 degrees maximum being the norm out of consideration of passenger comfort.

RPK: Revenue Passengers Kilometers

Paying Passengers multiplied by Kilometers flown by them. FTK (Freight Tons Kilometer) is the equivalent term for freight.

RSA: Runway Safety Area

Obstacle-free space beyond the runway to allow for overruns (and landing short). With airports encroaching on cities and vice-versa, these are not always as extensive as they should be. See Overruns.

Rudder

Control surface behind the tail fin (vertical stabilizer) that makes the aircraft yaw (turn) to the left or right.

Ruddervators/V-Tail

Empennage (tail assembly) where the traditional rudder and elevators are combined in a V-shape. Control system is complex and therefore rarely used. Main advantage is a military one in that the radar echo is reflected at an angle. Used in F-117 Nighthawk Stealth Fighter and the MQ Predator UAV (inverted V-tail).

Runway

Runways are designated according to their orientation in tens of degrees and whether they are the left one or the right one, or even the center one. Thus a left-hand runway pointing due East (90 degrees) would be Runway 09L. The parallel middle one would be 09C, and the right-hand one 09R.

Of course, as runways can work in opposite directions, so runway 09L approached from the other end would be (180 + 90 = 270 degrees), and designated 27R. These designations are marked at the beginning of each runway.

The length of runway an airliner needs to take off depends on the temperature and elevation—the higher and the hotter the location the greater the length of runway required.

Dallas-Fort Worth with seven runways and more planned, has some very long runways for this reason, with four being 13,400 ft (4,085 meters) long. JFK is famous amongst non-military facilities for its 14,752 ft (4,441 meter) 13R-31L runway, which being at sea level is 'worth' rather more than the equivalent length would be at DFW.

Major airports in Europe, such as Paris' Charles de Gaulle and Frankfurt have runways approximately 13,829 ft (4,215 meter) long. London's Heathrow's longest runway is merely 12,802 ft (3,902 meters) long despite it being the world's busiest international airport. Some people hope that if, as now seems unlikely, a new runway is eventually built, it could be full length like those at Paris and Frankfurt.

Runway Overruns

With improved warning and navigational equipment, such as GPS and terrain databases showing the height of the terrain ahead, the incidence of CFIT (Controlled Flight into Terrain) accidents has fallen, as have other accidents brought about by mechanical failure (thanks to greater reliability). As a result, runway overruns are featuring more and more in the accidents that do happen. These are often caused by a combination of factors including bad weather and landing too far down the runway. In the recent past a few cases terrible disasters were avoided thanks to good luck. This has not always been the case more recently. Constricted airports with inadequate overrun space are dangerous in this respect. See Overrun.

Runway Visual Range: RVR

Distance that can be seen looking down the runway and a key element in determining whether a given aircraft can land. Constantly reported to ATC controllers and pilots, nowadays by means of automatic equipment.

Ryanair

Low-cost airline, similar to easyJet and JetBlue, except that it often flies to cheaper airports located far from the cities designated as the destination and hence less appealing to businessmen.

Like easyJet, it came into a lot of flak regarding its advertising and Website showing cost of flight without extras such as airport taxes. According to an article by Ben Webster in the London Times, with tickets often so cheap, one in ten Ryanair passengers fails to turn up for their flight with the airline holding onto the sum paid as tax, etc. Even more than for easyJet, its success depends on trimming every possible cost. Would like to persuade passengers to only have carry-on luggage and check in online.

Ryanair has resorted to all sorts of devices to add extra charges when clients are booking online, that only someone well versed in the system and taking exceptional care would be able to avoid. This included (at the time of writing) a high card-processing fee *per person per flight* that could only be avoided by using an obscure payment card that hardly anyone would ever use. Since the airline would process all the charges together, their cost is very low, while the cost to say a family of four booking a return trip would be relatively extortionate. See Drip Pricing.

RSA: Runway Safety Area

According to the FAA, commercial airport runways should have an area 1,000 ft long and 500 ft wide beyond them to allow for overruns. However, many existing airports cannot meet this 'requirement' because of encroaching suburbia and other reasons. See EMAS.

RVR: Runway Visual Range

Visibility measured along the runway used as an indication as to whether possible to land or take off. Used to be measured by humans, but now done automatically unless equipment fails or airfield so small it lacks such equipment.

Sabotage (first proven case)

The first proven case of sabotage of an airliner was on October 10, 1933, when an explosive device very likely in the luggage compartment brought down a Boeing 247 operated by United Air Lines. It blew off the tail found virtually intact a mile away from the main debris. The explosive seemed to have been nitroglycerine.

The aircraft was on the Cleveland to Chicago leg of a transcontinental flight originating in Newark in New Jersey and bound for Oakland in California. The actual crash was near Chesterton, Indiana. The four passengers and three crew lost their lives.

Investigators could not even find a suspect, and why this came about remains a mystery.

Safest Airline

For many years, Australia's Qantas has been able to exploit the implication that they are the safest airline because they have never suffered a hull-loss, though recently a number of incidents have led to doubts being expressed in the media.

Qantas is relatively unique:

- In that Australia is a long way from almost anywhere and many of its flights are long-haul which means relatively few takeoffs and landings—the time accidents are most likely to occur.

- The airports used tend to be major ones where accidents are least likely.

- Compared with say American Airlines or United Airlines flying to all sorts of locations, Qantas is a relatively small operation, so it is easy to see that with a little bit of luck they could much more easily avoid suffering a major disaster.

  This little bit of good luck came into play in 1999, when *Qantas One*—a 747 flight from Sydney to London—overran the runway at 100 miles per hour (160 km/h) on landing at its intermediate stop, Bangkok . Luckily, the water-laden soil beyond the runway brought the careering jumbo to a stop before it hit an unforgiving obstacle, in which case it might have caught fire.

Safest Seat

What is the safest seat? is the question most often asked, though choice of airline and number of stopovers is more likely to determine one's longevity. However, once committed to taking a given flight it is worth knowing that statistics show that

- Those sitting within six or seven rows of an exit are more likely to survive a crash;

- An aisle seat is a safer option, rather than a window seat (where you risk having someone almost incapable of moving separating you from the aisle!);

- It is said by the experts that nowadays the few accidents that do happen vary so much in nature that it is impossible to say what section of the aircraft is safest.

That said, it has been found that survival can depend very much on preparedness, degree of mobility, and determination. The fact that passengers sitting at the front in First and Business would tend to be older than those at the back in Coach (Economy) could distort the figures. See Brace Position.

Safety

The study of accidents and their avoidance is a fascinating subject demanding expertise in domains ranging from psychology and sociology through Information Technology to Management. The French even have coined the word *Accidentologie*.

Theories and models such as those propounded by Professors Reason and Perrow, often devised in the context of the nuclear power industry where an accident could have terrible implications, are being applied to aviation where the implications are much more limited.

Screening of Passengers, Luggage & Freight

Surprisingly few accidents have been attributed to passenger ignorance, such as inadvertently bringing dangerous items on board. A notable case that could have led to a disaster was a pilgrim found attempting to light her cooking stove on a Pakistan Airlines flight. There was also a fire on a Taiwanese airliner fed by fuel in hand baggage in overhead lockers—thankfully with the aircraft on the ground.

Nowadays the greatest danger with regard to what passengers bring on relates to dangerous items brought intentionally on board, either to blow up the aircraft or to hijack it with the possible intention of using it as a flying bomb. With aircraft and systems generally becoming safer and safer, the fate of today's passenger may depend mostly on security measures, and consequently passenger screening has become a key facet of every flight.

Often the screening begins even before the passenger reaches the airport, in the form of checking names against watch lists. In the case of U.S.-bound flights, names of passengers and certain details have to be sent to the U.S. before departure. If the passenger happens to have the same name as someone on a watch list, they may have to undergo extensive questioning, or worse, leading to them missing their flight. This has resulted in absurd situations, with seven-year old boys being treated as potential hijackers—in one case the boy finally had to have an official insert in his passport certifying he was "OK" to prevent him being stopped every time.

Screening also takes place as passengers enter the airport, with their demeanor and even their route being taken into account. Some of the techniques used are not new. Many years ago, the French customs at Paris'

Orly Airport arranged customs channels so that smugglers would tend to choose a particular one and be more easily picked up.

With "terrorists" able to devise all sorts of ways to defeat the physical examination of baggage and persons before boarding, the authorities may well find themselves fighting the last war rather than the present one. For instance, after the shoe-bomber incident much attention has been paid to checking people's shoes even though terrorists are unlikely to use the same method again.

Many believe the terrorists will always be one step ahead, and so at airports and elsewhere great efforts are being made to develop software programs to identify automatically suspicious behavior using CCTV (Closed Circuit Television), heartbeat measurements and so on. While the CCTV can identify suspicious behavior such as *lurking with intent* in shopping malls, actually would be useful in the aircraft itself and is being considered, there is a long way to go before reliable systems can be developed.

SD: System Display

Seat Belts

With the almost universal adoption of seat belts in the case of road vehicles, they are now given scant attention. However, seat belts in airliners differ from their terrestrial versions in that the clasp has to be lifted, rather than pressed, to open them. It is thought that panicking passengers might regress mentally to what they were accustomed to doing every day. In the Habsheim air show crash, a young girl perished because she did not know how to unbuckle her seat belt. See AirBags.

Seats

Passenger seats have evolved, but while those in First and Business class have made spectacular improvements, including allowing the occupant to lie horizontally as if in a bed, those in Coach (Economy) have not done so. Of course, the latter have to be uncomfortable enough to make purchasing a more expensive ticket worthwhile.

While keeping to a conventional Economy Class layout, Air New Zealand are introducing a new type of seat where a platform rises up where the passenger's lower legs and feet would be, so that with three seats and the arm rests raised a couple can sleep as if on a bed. The airline will charge extra for this facility, but nothing like what they would charge for Business Class. In the case of adults, it would mean two people occupying three seats; in the case of two children, an extra seat might not be required. Passengers unable to share a berth may not be so happy, but then they might be on business and able to travel in Business Class.

At first sight, rearwards-facing seats would seem more logical as they should provide greater safety in the event of a crash with considerable backwards acceleration (forwards deceleration). Airlines have been reluctant to do this for a number of reasons, including

- They could impose too great a stress on existing cabin flooring.

- Stronger and hence heavier seats would be required which coupled with the strengthened attachments and stronger floor would mean a weight penalty.

- They could be less effective in accidents in which the main deceleration force is not along the longitudinal axis of the aircraft.

- They could expose occupants to the risk of injury from loose objects in an accident. These would strike occupants on the face or upper body rather than the back of their seat.

- Great improvements have been made in the design and construction of forward-facing seats.

- That they may not be suitable for use in modern jet transports with their high climb-out angles and that they could be psychologically less attractive to passengers. (By deploying the Spoilers, pilots can descend in normal circumstances without pushing the nose steeply downwards; however, to climb steeply they have to point it sharply upwards.)

Seat Pitch

Seat pitch is the distance between a given point on an airline seat to the equivalent point on the seat behind or in front.

The simplest way to measure seat pitch is from the back of the headrest to the back of the headrest of the seat in front or behind. This generally accepted way to define seat pitch gives an indication of the degree of (dis) comfort and the airline can easily calculate the number of rows that can be squeezed in.

However, the thickness of the seatback eats into the space available to the passenger. Therefore, bearing mind the increasing size of passengers, the U.K.'s CAA sets a minimum of 26 inches for the distance from where a person's lower back nestles against their seatback to the somewhat higher point on the seat in front (roughly where the food tray would be attached). Thus the 26-inch CAA seat pitch mentioned above would be equivalent an airline-defined seat pitch of about 27-28in, depending on the thickness of the back of the seat.

Air France have introduced a supplement of £40 for the prized seats with extra legroom in emergency-exit rows and at the front of the cabin on certain long-haul flights, and it seems other airlines have similar intentions. This extra charge will not apply to frequent flier cardholders with Gold or Platinum status, but to achieve that status many might be flying in business class anyway.

SELCL: Selective Calling System

Self-Healing

Now that Composites are being increasingly used in the construction of aircraft thought is being given to the idea of making the aircraft self-healing like the human body on suffering injuries—in fact aircraft suffer minor damage from all sorts of things—hailstones and even from knocks from vehicles and equipment when parked.

One idea is to include hollow fibers with a resin that would seep out and repair the damage. It would include a dye visible in ultra-violet light to help maintenance check on it later. Going even further, there could be a resin circulatory system that could be topped up as needed rather like a blood transfusion.

Separation

Distance maintained between aircraft. See Flight Levels.

SHM: Structural Health Monitoring

SHM is an emerging technology whereby systems, such as sensor-actuator networks, might automatically assess the integrity of aircraft structures. According to *Flight International*, Airbus views SHM as a key to its *intelligent structure philosophy* and Boeing sees it as an emerging technology that may provide significant improvements in operational efficiencies.

It is rather as if an aircraft had a nervous system like a human, able to tell when and where something was hurting. With increasing use of (non-conductive) composite materials that are intrinsically more difficult to check during maintenance such monitoring could be invaluable.

Shoe bomber (Richard Reid)

One unexpected advantage of the no-smoking rule in airliners is that it makes anyone trying to light some primitive explosive device more obvious.

The was exemplified by the case of Richard Reid, the shoe bomber, who was found trying to light an explosive device in the heel of his very large shoe on American Airlines Flight AA63 from Paris to Miami December 22, 2001. It only failed to detonate because airport security in Paris had detained him the previous day, and moisture from his sweat and the air overnight had made the fuse too damp.

Airport security had prevented 6 foot 4 inch (193 cm) Reid from boarding a flight the previous day because of his disheveled appearance and lack of check-in luggage. He had been handed over to the French National Police who finally gave him the all clear and the AA ticket to Miami. He duly passed through the screening process, which at the time ignored people's footwear.

It was after meal service that a flight attendant thought she smelt a match and went to see if someone was lighting up. A passenger indicated it was Reid, sitting alone, and she duly told him smoking was not permitted. He promised to comply, but a short while later she was annoyed to see him in a huddled position as if hiding something, which she thought might be a cigarette. He remained huddled and did not respond when she asked him what he was doing.

When she approached even closer and insisted, Reid tried to ward her off, incidentally revealing his lap where he had a shoe with a fuse he was trying to light. She called for help with Reid wrestling her to the floor. With another female flight attendant joining the fray, she was able to slither away and get some water, which she brought back and threw in Reid's face. Passengers by then had come to the assistance of the second flight attendant who had been bitten by Reid.

Reid was subdued, tied up and given a sedative by a physician who happened as usual to be on board. It was then she saw he had a shoe in his lap and seemed to be trying to light it. The aircraft was then diverted to Boston's Logon International Airport where Reid was arrested.

Though the timely actions of the flight attendant are reported as having prevented all 198 persons on board that flight from being killed, one could say Paris Airport Security had prevented a disaster. Had it not been for their suspicions the previous day having resulted in Reid wearing those shoes for 24 hours and the fuse becoming too damp to light, the device would have gone off almost without fail on a Miami bound flight the previous day.

Reid was sentenced to a long term of imprisonment with the recent relaxation of his jail conditions being contentious, but first, does his case have any lessons regarding what makes someone want to kill 198 people including themselves?

Reid had a difficult childhood, with his father, a Jamaican, spending much of it in prison. His mother was English. He was involved in petty crime, and in and out of young offenders' facilities. He became a Muslim on the advice of his father who said Muslims were treated better and got better food. The young Reid had to feeling of being discriminated against, attended a mosque where extremist views were prevalent, and began to express more and more extremist views himself. It was then that a scout probably identified him suicide bomber material.

The recent easing of the conditions of Reid's incarceration in a maximum-security jail has been a matter of some contention. Initially strict limits were placed regarding with whom he could contact and associate. However, in view of the provisions of the U.S. Constitution regarding religious freedom, and the present Administration's more legalistic stance, lawyers have successfully managed to get these relaxed, with the result that even extremists at the prison such as Reid can associate there and pray together.

In an interview, Reid has said

"Of course, I would have been sad to have those people die, but I knew that my cause was just and righteous. It was the will of Allah that I did not succeed."

Showers (on board)

Emirates (Airlines) have installed a couple of showers in First Class on their new Airbus 380s and had hoped to re-use the water for hand washing—after filtering and treatment with ultra-violet light—but could not get approval from the European authorities, despite tests showing there should be no problem. As a result, the aircraft will have to carry extra water required with the showers timed to last no longer than 5 minutes.

Aircraft toilets nowadays are very sophisticated using vacuum flushing and very little water. This has the advantage that they can use narrow-bore piping and be installed more flexibly with less danger of leakages damaging the aircraft over time. Leakage of water, even from the galleys, can be dangerous as it can cause corrosion or cause avionics or electrical systems to malfunction.

Side Stick: Side Stick Controller (SSC)

Feature of Airbus cockpits where the traditional control column between the pilot's legs is replaced by a control stick rather like one for playing computer games at their side close to the outer wall. Thus, the captain sitting on the left has to use his left hand, whereas the copilot sitting on the right uses his right hand.

Sideslip

Dipping a wing when not performing a turn causes the aircraft to slip sideways. A sideslip is frequently used to compensate at the last minute for a crosswind when landing (see Crab). Glider pilots are experts at using sideslips to lose height as shown in the Gimli Glider fuel depletion incident in Canada.

SIGINT: Signals Intelligence

Intelligence gathered through the capture and analysis of messages between people (COMINT—communications intelligence) and/or between machines (e.g. ELINT—electronic intelligence). As SIGINT is sometimes used to refer to COMINT there is room for confusion.

Sometimes an innocent aircraft might purposely be flown close to a potential enemy's facilities to provoke a response for SIGINT and radar emission analysis.

Sigmet: Significant Meteorological Information

Warning issued by aviation meteorological service about suddenly deteriorating weather conditions.

Skidding and Sideslipping

If rudder is applied without any banking, the aircraft will skid outwards. Conversely, if the aircraft is banked without any rudder input, it will sideslip in the direction of the wing that is lower.

Usually, by Coordinating operation of rudder, ailerons and elevators, the aircraft can be made to turn without either happening and the passengers feeling their weight is going straight down (but not actually downwards to Earth) onto their seats.

Occasionally, a sideslip is done purposely to lose height, such as when an aircraft runs out of fuel and must make lose height gliding to its landing point because it cannot go around. See Gimli Glider and 80-Mile Glide in *Air Crashes and Miracle Landings.*

SKYbrary (http://www.skybrary.aero)

Safety knowledge provided by EUROCONROL, ICAO and the Flight Safety Foundation.

A site for exchange of safety information—a kind of air *safety library.* Well worth looking at and contributing to.

Slant Distance

Line-of-sight (hypotenuse) distance to a beacon taking into account both vertical and horizontal distance. Thus, an aircraft directly above a radio beacon at 1,000ft agl would be 1,000ft away as regards the slant distance! See DME.

Slot

The narrow meaning is the allocated take off time from an airport and agreed with ATC. The late boarding of some passengers can result in the slot being missed and the need to request a new one. This can result in a long wait not only because of congestion at the airport in question, but also because permission may be required to overfly zones thousands of miles away.

The wider meaning of slot is the right for an airline to fly from an airport within a certain time frame (and in turn, at a certain time). At popular airports such as London's Heathrow, the slots are very valuable due to their limited number, and an airline possessing many slots such as British Airways is in a very enviable position commercially. See Open Skies Agreement.

Smith, Patrick (salon.com)

See *Ask The Pilot.*

SMS: Safety Management Systems

A proactive systematic approaches and programs for improving safety in fields such as maintenance, airport management and so on.

Accidents cited as ones that might have been avoided had SMS been employed include the Milan-Linate accident where a straying Cessna wandered into the path of an airliner taking off and the Taipei accident where a Singapore Airlines aircraft mistakenly took off from a disused runway and collided with construction equipment parked on it.

Speed Tape

With the introduction of LCD displays, information can be presented graphically in a more understandable way together with other information. For instance, instead of primarily relying on a traditional separate Air Speed Indicator with hands like a clock, one can incorporate a Speed Tape in the Primary Flight Display. This is a simulated vertical tape like that of a tape measure indicating airspeed. Not only is it easier to comprehend, but can have marks (Bugs) on it showing desired speed, reference speed for landing, maximum speed, and so on.

Spoilers

Spoilers are flat panels inlaid on top of the wings and hinged at the front, which are flicked up to 'spoil' the flow of air over the wing. This not only produces an air braking effect, but also increase the sink rate, enabling the aircraft to lose height without pointing the nose downwards. Deployed automatically as soon as the main wheels touch the runway on landing, they lessen the aircraft's tendency to bounce and furthermore push the tires harder down on the runway thus improving grip as the wheel brakes are applied. Their air-braking effect quickly falls away as the aircraft slows.

Spot Height

Elevation (height above mean sea level) of high points (mountain peaks, buildings, etc.) shown on aviation charts, and in the case of towers and buildings with the height agl in brackets underneath.

Squawk

Reply from transponder on aircraft with limited amount of information shown on ATC controller's screen when probed by radar. Shows a code in addition to the aircraft's identity and height—unlike military radar (primary radar) designed to detect 'intruders', most ATC radar is secondary radar and depends on the transponder to tell it the height of the aircraft as determined by the aircraft's barometric altimeter. If that altimeter is wrong, the height indicated to ATC will be wrong too.

The term *squawk* comes from the Second World War when the transponder was first installed as an IFF (Identification of Friend or Foe) device, and given the codename *Parrot.* Turning it on (to indicate one was a friend) was called *squawking.* The name stuck. See the more obvious Squirt.

Squirt

Term used for the burst of very comprehensive data/info given out by devices such as ADS-B transponders.

SSR: Secondary Surveillance Radar

Typical Radar used by ATC identifying aircraft from the signal <u>emitted by their transponders</u>.

It can see their direction and distance, but unlike Primary Radar (such as used by the military for detecting an enemy) Secondary Radar depends on the aircraft transponder to ascertain height. This is something that the pilots of the Peruvian airliner with misbehaving instruments failed to realize when told by ATC that they were at 9,700 ft just when they were about to crash into the sea. [An aircraft cleaner had left duct tape over the Pitot tube inlets so altitude and airspeed readings in the aircraft were erroneous.]

Stabilized Approach

For safety reasons, both the military and airlines insist pilots have their aircraft lined up with the runway in good time, at the appropriate speed and with the correct flap setting.

Pilots, especially of low-cost carriers with short turnaround times where minimal delay on arrival is high on their management's agenda, can feel pressured into making last minute maneuvers to avoid a lengthy go-around after a bad approach that might reflect on them. At least one such carrier has taken steps to ensure this is not the case.

Stall

Loss of ability to fly due to too low an airspeed or a change in flaps setting meaning the wing can no longer provide lift at the given airspeed.

As the onset of a stall can be very sudden, manufacturers install sensors to detect signs of abnormal airflow over the wings and warn the pilots of an imminent stall. The warning can take various forms, including sound, verbal warnings and shaking of the control column.

In traditional aircraft with the engine(s) mounted on the nose or the wings, and with a low tail assembly, the nose drops of its own accord in a stall, thereby helping the aircraft regain enough speed to recover. However, in high tail aircraft with engines at the rear, the opposite happens—the nose goes up inducing an even greater decrease in airspeed in turn resulting in a catastrophic stall from which recovery *might* only be possible from a very considerable height.

To avoid this, aircraft with tail-mounted engines (as well as other aircraft) are equipped with systems (Stick Shakers, warning lights and audible alerts) to WARN pilots of an imminent stall. Should those fail to make the pilot take corrective action, a Stick-Pusher finally pushes the nose down before the actual stall. The pilots override this at their peril.

While stalls usually occur due to a loss of airspeed—itself caused by insufficient thrust from the engines, climbing with insufficient power or say a headwind suddenly changing to a tailwind—they can happen at constant airspeeds in the event of say the flaps, droops or slats being (inadvertently) retracted. Such stalls are called Change of Configuration Stalls.

See Compressor Stall, which is something quite different. .

Static Pressure

The Static Pressure is the pressure of the air outside the aircraft when static (i.e. not being forced in or out due to motion of the aircraft through the air). The barometric altimeter depends on this. The airspeed is measured by having a pitot tube consisting of an open-ended tube pointing forwards with the air rushing into it, and comparing that pressure with the static pressure.

There was a tragic accident to a Peruvian airliner where an aircraft ports to prevent the entry of cleaning fluid. The aircraft took off with the polisher forgot to remove duct tape he had placed over the pitot and static instruments going wild and eventually crashed into the sea with the pilots thinking they were at 9,700 ft.

Static Wicks/Static Discharge Wicks

So-called wicks attached to trailing edges of wings, ailerons, elevators rudder, and vertical and horizontal stabilizer tips to discharge static electricity that could amongst other things impede operation of onboard navigation and communications systems. While they dissipate electric charges, they neither increase nor decrease the probability of a lightning strike. However, such strikes can damage them.

Sterile Cockpit Rule

The so-called Sterile Cockpit Rule was a regulation issued by the FAA in 1981 after a series of accidents attributed wholly or in part to pilots being distracted during critical phases of the flight. Such distractions included idle chatter, visits from cabin crew, and intercom calls from cabin crew.

Critical phases included taxiing and flight up to 10,000ft. Passengers will often hear a "chime" when the aircraft reaches 10,000ft telling the flight attendants the pilots are out of quarantine!

The use of reinforced cockpit doors and restrictions concerning entry to the flight deck introduced in the aftermath of Nine-Eleven mean greater sterility. Some maintain this has the disadvantage of making it even more difficult for the aircrew and cabin crew to bond and work together in the CRM context in an emergency.

There was the Colgan regional carrier crash in which the pilots allowed the airspeed to drop dangerously, and the captain reacted inappropriately (in panic) to the Stick Shaker indicating a Stall by raising the nose. The

NTSB noted the pilots had been gossiping for most of the flight, thereby infringing sterile cockpit rules, and carried out procedures late as a result.

Stick-shaker

To warn pilots of an imminent stall the control column may be made to shake artificially. Many other means of warning pilots of such a possibility usually come into play. A number of aircraft have automatic recovery programs. See Alpha-Floor.

Straight-in (Landing)

A landing where the aircraft comes straight in without joining a rectangular pattern. See Base Leg and Downwind Leg.

Structural Health Monitoring (SHM)

Use of sensors, etc. to monitor structural state of the aircraft, especially where composite materials that cannot be checked in the traditional ways are involved.

Subsonic Flight

When an aircraft is flying below the speed of sound, *info* moves forward through the air enabling it to start moving aside even before encountering say a leading edge. At and beyond the speed of sound this is no longer the case and the air slams against the leading edges creating a shockwave. This is the so-called *sound barrier*, which was once the subject of movies with pilots risking their lives to break it.

In practice everything is not so cut and dried, as the contours of an aircraft, say a thick wing with a considerable bulge on top, means that the speed of the air differs from one place to another, and one part of the aircraft may be flying sub-sonically and another part supersonically. The term *transonic* is applied to the range of speeds between pure subsonic flight and pure supersonic flight—roughly Mach 0.8-0.85 to Mach 1.15-1.2).

Supersonic Flight (>Mach 1)

As mentioned under Mach, drag and problems increase sharply as the aircraft approaches the speed of sound. Airliners cruise at around Mach 8.5 since marginal gains in speed would not be worth the extra cost.

Interestingly, there is another barrier that is again financial rather than technical, namely that above Mach 2.2, the heat generated by the compression of the air molecules surrounding the aircraft becomes so great (despite the bitterly cold temperatures at the operating height) that special heat-resistant materials are required. That is why the Anglo-French supersonic Concorde had a cruising speed around Mach 2, and a maximum speed near Mach 2.2.

As no other aircraft would be flying up to almost 60,000 ft, Concorde was able to perform a continuous climb (rather than the usual step climb) and fly at the optimum height for the weight of fuel remaining.

Supersonic Transport (SST)

Faced with Russia's apparent lead in the Space exploration, President Kennedy initiated the Apollo program, which succeeded in putting Americans on the moon and luckily bringing them back. Faced with the danger of the U.S. being beaten in the aviation sphere by the Europeans with their supersonic Concorde airliner, Kennedy in 1963 also initiated a project to design an airliner that would beat the European craft hands down by flying at three times the speed of sound.

Boeing was awarded the contract, but found it something of a poisoned chalice as though largely funded by Washington, it took resources away from other projects such as the 747. In 1971, Congress voted to cancel the project, which was opposed by many for diverse reasons including noise and the alleged danger of cancer due to the effect of damage to the upper atmosphere. Interestingly, there is now mention of "Advanced concept studies for Supersonic Commercial Transport Aircraft Entering Service in the 2018-2020 Period",

Swiss Cheese Accident Model

Concept conceived by Professor James Reason, whose book *Human Error* (1990). New York: Cambridge University Press and other work revolutionized the way accidents are analyzed, with the causes being sought throughout the system even where the acts of the operators (for instance the pilots) not appropriate—due perhaps to bad training.

The Swiss Cheese Model seems very simple in that the idea is that there are various layers in a system or organization:

- Organizational Influences (Latent Failures)
- Unsafe Supervision (Latent Failures)
- Preconditions for Unsafe Acts (Latent and/or Active Failures
- Unsafe Acts (Active Failures) [say by pilots]

If the holes in each layer (in the cheese) coincide, allowing a knitting needle to pass through, the result will be an ACCIDENT. This is an oversimplification, and there is much more to Professor Reason's work than that.

Some say that while the Reason model is good for looking at accidents retroactively, it is not so good for finding the failures proactively. Thus, the ICAO recommends use of the SHEL model.

See Normal Accident (Prof. Perrow) and Judgment Errors (Wiegmann and Shappell).

TACAN: Tactical Air Navigation

U.S. term for a VOR air navigation beacon for military use. More accurate than the civilian one, but less valuable now we have GPS.

A U.S. military aircraft reporting the location of the crash site of JL123 in I Japan in 1985 gave the TACAN bearing and distance.

Taking off (Critical V-Speeds)

At take-off (and at other times) there are various critical speeds (velocities). Having the appropriate airspeed is life or death for an aircraft, as it is the forward **air**speed that provides the lift.

- Takeoff Decision Speed (V_1)

  As the aircraft accelerates down the runway, the pilots are constantly checking that all systems are "GO" and are ready to abort the take off should a significant problem manifest itself. This is always a nervous moment, but less so now that engines are more reliable and have power to spare. The pilots can abort the take off at any time right up to the *take off decision speed* (V_1). Thereafter they are committed, and have to proceed with the take off almost regardless of what goes wrong.

  This commitment to pursue the takeoff regardless is not as frightening as it might seem, as having reached the decision speed the aircraft should be able to take off safely even if an engine fails, say through ingestion of a large bird or a flock of birds.

  Aborting the take-off after attaining V_1 could well result in the aircraft being unable to stop before reaching the end of the runway, and slamming into unforgiving objects beyond, and is a No! No! It is similar to a car driver approaching green traffic lights that may change to amber, in that the driver is initially prepared to stop, but gets to a point where it is dangerous to try to do so.

- Rotation Speed (V_R)

  The next critical speed on takeoff is the so-called *rotation speed* V_R. It is slightly higher than the decision speed V_1, and is the speed at which the pilot gently pulls back on the control column or side stick, so the aircraft rotates in the vertical plane. The nose rises with the pilots taking care that is does not rise so much that the rear of the fuselage strikes the ground. The angle at which the wings encounter the oncoming air, called the *angle of attack or* α (at Airbus), increases so that the wings facing slightly upwards lift the aircraft into the air.

  Though the aircraft would be able to lift off before V_R, the pilots do not attempt to do so. This is to ensure they have a sufficient margin of speed to allow for sudden changes in wind speed/direction that might cause one wing to stall (lose lift) resulting in the aircraft tilting to one side with an engine or wingtip striking the ground. In addition, the airspeed must be high enough for the rudder to be able to correct a major yaw caused by failure of an engine, say due to ingestion of birds.

- Takeoff Safety Speed (V_2)

  Once the aircraft is properly airborne (reckoned to be 35ft above ground) under takeoff power, the next critical speed is the *take-off safety speed* (V_2) which is the minimum speed permitted by the airline for climbing away.

  Its purpose is to avoid the pilots cutting back too much on engine power in complying with noise-abatement procedures. Again, it incorporates a good safety margin to allow for the previously mentioned possible sudden changes in wind direction.

Typical V-Speeds

It is the norm in aviation to give all speeds in knots (nautical miles per hour). A Knot is about 1.15 mph or 1.85 k/h., so to convert to miles or kilometers merely entails adding on 15% or 85% respectively.

For a Boeing 747-400 weighing 800,000 lb (363 tonnes) with flaps at an angle of 20 degrees

V_1 might be of the order of 153 knots (175mph/283kph)

V_R slightly higher at around 169 knots (194mph/312kph)

V_2 might be 181 knots (208mph/334kph)

Taking off (Flap and Slat settings)

When an aircraft is taking off (and landing), *flaps* on the wings are extended downwards at an angle at the rear of the wings to increase lift at low speeds. Most aircraft in addition now have movable *slats* on the leading edges of the wings to prevent stalling and give extra lift at slow speeds.

The awful takeoff crash at Madrid in 2008 was very likely caused by the failure of the non-deployment of flaps warning system to work—one of the simplest things.

Taxiing (from Gate to the runway)

The *push back* or *pull back* is a procedure whereby a Tractor pushes or pulls the aircraft away from the (boarding) *gate*. The aircraft then taxies to the runway for takeoff, or more usually to a holding point, so that it does not enter a runway on which another aircraft may be taking off or landing. With increasing congestion at airports, taxiing is potentially a very dangerous part of the flight, and especially so in bad visibility. Having the aircraft possibly fully laden with the fuel required for a long flight adds to the danger. Nevertheless, ground collisions are now exceedingly rare due to the lessons learnt from disasters described here.

If an aircraft enters a runway by mistake, it is called a *runway incursion*, and is considered very serious as an aircraft that is landing, or that is taking off from a point further back on the runway may hit it.

Taxiing (from Runway to Gate)

Runways generally have a number of exits, and nowadays automatic braking systems can help pilots reach the appropriate exit at the right speed. Should an aircraft have to linger on the runway perhaps due to touching down too far from the threshold, the controller may have to order the following aircraft to go around, even though in all likelihood the aircraft will have cleared the runway by the time it actually touches down itself. This seems to happen not infrequently at Tokyo's Narita airport, with passengers saying how dangerous it had been when it was nothing of the sort and just a precaution.

The last few yards to the Gate are facilitated by indications from a member of the ground staff so the aircraft comes to a halt at just the right spot.

TCAS: Traffic Alert & Collision Avoidance System

System whereby dedicated computers in nearby aircraft liaise with each other and warn pilots of the presence of nearby traffic. In the event of risk of collision, mandatory instructions are given to the respective pilots so they move their aircraft away and not towards each other. TCAS instructions take precedence over all others including those of air traffic controller. Though the technology was developed in the 1960s, it was only in the early nineties that it became the norm for airliners—after a spate of mid-air collisions and near misses.

It is obviously better if both aircraft on a collision course have TCAS, and can both take mutually appropriate avoiding action. However, a TCAS equipped aircraft with a Mode C transponder (installed in virtually all aircraft allowed to fly in the vicinity of major airports in the U.S.), is able to tell its pilots how it thinks the other not so equipped aircraft should be avoided. Pilots also use TCAS on the ground to alert them of the presence of other aircraft close-by (say on runway in bad visibility when taking off).

TCDS: Type Certificate Data Sheets (FAA)

"The Type Certificate Data Sheets (TCDS) database is a repository of Make and Model information. The TCDS is a formal description of the aircraft, engine or propeller. It lists limitations and information required for type certification including airspeed limits, weight limits, thrust limitations, etc."

Terrorist Talent Spotters

Just as corporations, government agencies, intelligence agencies, and the like, have spotters looking out for people with special talents, terrorist organization have their agents looking out for people with religious fervor, grievances or a sense that injustices are being committed, and who therefore can be exploited. The Shoe Bomber, Richard Reid, is thought to have come to the attention of one such spotter.

One easy prey for such spotters has been the children of Pakistanis living in the U.K. sent back to Pakistan by their desperate parents hoping that a rehab in a religious madrassa would enable them to kick their drug dependency.

Thales

Thales is the rebranded French Thomson-CSF following its acquisition of the U.K.'s Racal Electronics. The name reflects its increasing international presence and aspirations. Indeed, it has become one of the World's top ten defense-electronics companies.

More than half its business is defense-related with the company's reach even extending to shipbuilding. This includes working with Britain's BAE on the design of future aircraft carriers.

Described by Janes, as a France-based *systems house* with one intention being to position itself as the hub of a European counterweight to U.S. dominance in the unmanned aerial vehicle (UAV) market.

Their buzzword is *mission-critical,* applied to any project, even civilian. Stress dual use, in the sense that expertise gained in domain of military technology can be applied in the civilian context—even for something quite mundane.

Operating in a similar environment to Britain's BAE, there have similarly been questions raised concerning the means used to obtain contracts.

Thales is doing a great deal of business with Airbus, and will be doing even more in areas such as flight entertainment systems and more importantly avionics where large sums will be involved. The relationship could have been much more formal had the Germans not in late 2004 blocked Mr. Fourgeard's plan for Thales to integrate with EADS. The German side feared this would give the French too much weight—a constant fear.

Thermals

Updrafts of air that sometimes cause aircraft to rise up uncomfortably. Birds and gliders love them. What passengers call *air pockets*, where the aircraft seems to be falling relentlessly, are not pockets at all, but simply down drafts.

Threshold

To allow a safety margin, aircraft do not land right at the start of the concrete runway, but at a point somewhat beyond defined as the *Threshold.* In fact, they usually land just beyond rather like stepping over the threshold into someone's house.

A *Displaced Threshold* is the rare case where the threshold is not right at the beginning of the runway because of the proximity of buildings or a hill.

Sometimes the threshold is displaced because the runway at the original threshold has become weakened due to the impact of repetitive landings. Though a displaced threshold means less runway is available, that only applies to landings as the entire runway can be used for takeoffs.

Thrust Vectoring
Method to increase the maneuverability of fighter aircraft by supplementing control surface directional input with input achieved by diverting the thrust from the engine or engines. Found in fifth generation fighters such as the Mig-35 and the F-22 Raptor.

Tilt Rotor Helicopter
These are helicopter with rotors that tilt through 90°, combining the advantages of the traditional helicopter with those of a fixed wing aircraft, to allow much greater horizontal speed. See Helicopter.

Titanium
Metal with the best strength to weight ratio increasingly used in aircraft, after initially being mostly used for the engine components. Maintains strength at moderate temperatures. However, with extensive use in the latest airliners such as the A380 and particularly the Boeing 787, it is in short supply with its price increasing to the extent that alternatives are being sought where possible.

TOGA: Take-Off-Go-Around
An aircraft may have to abandon a landing for many reasons, including the presence of another aircraft on the runway or bad weather. For safety reasons, the incoming aircraft usually immediately applies full take-off power so it can recover airspeed and climb away rapidly. Modern aircraft have a TOGA button that will do what is necessary, though some pilots prefer to do the procedure manually to avoid scaring the passengers—the computer is programmed on the assumption that it might be a dangerous situation and applies sudden power accordingly.

TRACON: Terminal Radar Approach Control
ATC and Radar facility used for airspace from the airport up to a height of 18,000ft in the U.S. and a maximum distance of roughly 50 miles. Often referred to as Departure and Approach (Control).

Track
The actual path of aircraft over the ground taking into account drift caused by side wind.

Transponder
Initially developed in World War II as an IFF (Identification of Friend or Foe) device that would reply to show whether aircraft friendly when interrogated by radar. Nowadays transponders Squawk (transmit) aircraft height, flight number and Squawk Code indicating their situation—there

are special squawk codes for an emergency, hijack, etc. The latest transponders, called S-Mode Transponders Squirt (transmit) a whole stream of information including actual position determined by GPS, the maneuver (climbing, turning, etc.) being undertaken, thus making future collision avoidance theoretically much more effective.

Traffic Pattern

Aircraft fly very precise rectangular patterns around an airport prior to landing. Each side of the rectangle has a name. The leg flown parallel to the runway and opposite to the direction of landing is the Downwind Leg. The Base Leg, as it is known, is flown at right angles to the runway, just before turning to the final direction for landing. Traffic patterns may be flown with either right-hand or left-hand turns, though in the early days of aviation they were to the left and that is why the captain traditionally has the left-hand seat—so he can see where they are going on the turns.

Trident (Hawker Siddeley Trident) [1964] 117

British short- to medium-range airliner with three tail-mounted engines famous for selling in small numbers because specked according to the wishes of British European Airways (BEA). It was the first airliner able to perform blind landings (called Autoland) in commercial service. Many found service in China—perhaps because of price and because the BEA specification met China's needs too.

Trim (adjusting the trim)

Supplementary (mini-) control surfaces integrated with rudder, ailerons or elevators that can be adjusted so the aircraft flies naturally straight, with wings level, or even climbs or descends without pressure on control column (or Sidestick). Adjusting these to achieve the desired effect is called trimming.

Pilots taking over manual control from the autopilot have on occasions been disastrously caught out by presence of extreme trim that the computer has been applying to correct what it considers the wrong control column input, say by the other pilot. This happened in the case of a China Airlines Airbus landing at Nagoya in Japan.

TriStar (Lockheed L1101) [1972] 250

Excellent three-engine airliner developed by Lockheed in competition with the ill-fated McDonnell Douglas DC-10. It was destined for the medium to long-haul wide body market just below the high volume long-haul market grabbed by the Boeing 747.

Unfortunately, problems that Britain's Rolls Royce had in developing the new engine meant the aircraft arrived late on the market with the result that McDonnell Douglas—already well established as a supplier to the U.S. airlines—took the lead as regards orders. This was despite Lockheed being persuaded to offer sweeteners, which ultimately led to the resignation of the Japanese prime minister.

Thus, Lockheed never sold enough to make the venture profitable and indeed lost so much money that the company decided to pull out of civilian airliner production altogether.

TSA: Transportation Security Administration

Set up under the DHS (Department of Homeland Security) in the aftermath of Nine-Eleven. Though responsible for security in all transportation modes, it is in the aviation domain that it is most high profile.

It is responsible for screening passengers for dangerous or forbidden items, and in future, checking passengers against the *Watch Lists* of individuals deemed a threat. This task used to be largely the responsibility of the airlines. The FBI's Terrorist Screening Center (TSC), with the help of other, agencies draws up those watch lists.

Federal Air Marshall—armed officers travelling incognito on aircraft in the U.S. and abroad—come under its remit. They also have a program whereby some aircrew can be specially trained in the use of firearms and how to deal with onboard threats, and act in an unpaid capacity as an extra line of defense.

Like its counterparts in other countries, the TSA has been criticized for excessive rules about what passengers can carry on board an aircraft and for not concentrating on people who could be dangerous. It is adopting a more thoughtful approach and no longer hunting for nail-clippers.

See Behavior Detection Officers.

Turn and Bank Indicator

Instrument found even in the smallest GA aircraft. Indicates how the aircraft is banking and turning and whether the operation is coordinated—i.e. correct bank angle for the speed and rate of turn. See Coordinated Flight.

UAV: Unmanned Air Vehicle

A pilotless airliner, although said to be theoretically possible, is a long way off and is not likely to be popular with the public. One manufacturer is seriously examining a single pilot airliner concept while admitting there no enthusiasm for such an aircraft now among airlines. With increasing automation and easier navigation thanks to NextGen air traffic control systems, the manufacturer believes the main argument for having two pilots will only be the need to have a reserve should one fall ill.

However, the military are investing considerable funds in the development of usually very small pilotless air vehicles, such as the U.S. Predator, that thanks to modern technology can fly under their own GPS guidance systems or under remote control to gather intelligence (Sigint, photos, etc.) or even to attack small targets such as vehicles carrying persons to be *terminated*.

In its first investigation into an un-manned aircraft accident, the NTSB made 22 recommendations relating to the April 2006 U.S. Customs and Border Protection UAV crash in Arizona when the team piloting accidentally turned off its engine.

It is certain that the civilian use of UAVs poses many problems, with the danger that severely limiting their operations will make it difficult to exploit them to the full.

Ullage
Ullage is the space above a liquid in a container, such as the air above the wine in a wine bottle.

A British RAF Hercules was shot down by small arms fire in Iraq due to an explosive mixture forming in the ullage as the fuel was used up. Had the aircraft's wing tanks been fitted with ESP (Explosive Suppressant Foam) as recommended and as had been the case for U.S. Hercules since the sixties, the disaster could well have been avoided.

Undercarriage/Landing Gear
The often complex system between the body of the aircraft and the ground, allowing it to come down safely even with quite a thump, and to move over the ground, be steered and brought to a halt. U.S. pilots tend to favor the term *landing gear* as opposed to *undercarriage*. They will say *gear down* to confirm the undercarriage is down.

Most airliners have tricycle undercarriages, with the main weight carried by the main wheels under the wings, with a relatively tiny nose wheel to provide equilibrium and steering. See Crab, explaining how aircraft cope with crosswinds when landing, and how the B-52 bomber almost uniquely has an undercarriage that swivels.

Upgrade
At certain times, such as during holiday periods, many seats in Business Class are liable to remain unsold. Airlines used to upgrade Economy Class (Coach) passengers so as to be able to sell off the vacated Economy seats. A recent trend, especially in the U.S., has been to sell off these seats as Business Class at a good discount but well above the Economy fare.

U.S.A: United Space Alliance
This abbreviation is somewhat confusing in view of its close association with NASA which writes "U.S.A." on objects seen by the public, whether it be on the Moon or on Earth. Internally, NASA uses "U.S.A" to denote the United Space Alliance, a distinct entity based in Houston with Boeing and Lockheed working together, born out of NASA's desire to avoid dealing with too many individual contractors. Too many contractors, with their subcontractors, was thought to have been a factor in previous safety problems at NASA, and notably with regard to the Space Shuttle.

UTC: See Coordinated Universal Time/Zulu

The odd abbreviation UTC resulted from a face-saving compromise at the International Telecommunications Union, between those wanting

- Coordinated Universal Time [CUT]
- Temps Universel Coordonné [TUC]

Value of Human Life

See Cost Benefit

V-speeds

Airspeeds (velocities) of special significance—especially at takeoff and landing—calculated according to conditions such as the total weight of the aircraft, air temperature, and flap settings.

There are many V-speeds, referring to the airspeed at which the aircraft could do such and such. However, the key ones are

- **V_S:** Stalling Speed
- **V_1:** Takeoff Decision Speed

  Having reached this takeoff decision speed it should be possible to take off safely even in the event of the failure of an engine, and on reaching that speed, pilots are committed to pursuing the takeoff.

- **V_R:** Rotation Speed

  Speed at which pilots rotate (raise the nose) so the wings *provide the lift to takeoff.*

- *V_2: Takeoff Safety Speed*

  Airspeed that the aircraft must have attained on reaching a height of 35 ft. Pilots must ensure airspeed never falls below that, especially when reducing power in accordance with noise restrictions. Includes a safety factor to allow for deviations and wind changes.

- **V_{REF}:** Speed for Final Phase of a Landing

  Reference (desired) speed for landing calculated according to weight, flap settings, etc. Too slow and the aircraft might stall; too fast and the aircraft might not be able to land safely or land without enough runway remaining to stop safely. If actual airspeed deviates from V_{REF} by more than the company allows, say 20 knots, the pilots should abort the landing and go-around.

For typical Boeing 747 takeoff speeds, see Takeoff.

VASIS: Visual Approach Slope Indicator System

Array of directional lights near the touchdown point on the runway that appear to change color according to whether the pilot is below, on, or above the glide path.

VC10 (Vickers VC10) [1964] 54

The VC-10 was an excellent airliner with four tail-mounted engines. Sales failed to reach expectations because it was designed specifically to meet special requirements of BOAC. See Airbus History.

Vertical Speed

The vertical speed is the rate of ascent or descent.

The VSI (Vertical Speed Indicator) is one of the key instruments in all aircraft.

In modern aircraft, the computer issues a verbal warning *SINK RATE ... SINK ... RATE*, if it finds the rate of descent is dangerously high for the circumstances. Some aircraft such as the early Boeing 727s and 737s could be sinking irretrievably fast without the pilots realizing it—for very considerable engine power was required just to stay level with full flap.

VFR: Visual Flight Rules (as opposed to IFR)

The pilot must be flying in good visibility conditions and is responsible for seeing and avoiding other aircraft, towers, mountains, etc. A pilot may be flying under Instrument Flight Rules (IFR) even in good visibility.

VHF: Very High Frequency

A radio signal giving good quality line-of-sight transmissions, which means the signal can be blocked by mountains.

Used for VOR and short range radio communications.

Viscount (Vickers Viscount) [1950] 445

A British 4-engine turboprop airliner originally seating around 50 passengers, with a later version seating up to 71. Saw many years of service.

VOR: Very High Frequency Omni-directional Range

A radio beacon on the ground whose VHF radio signal enables aircraft to determine both distance (range) and compass bearing (radial) from it. Much more sophisticated but principle similar to lighthouses that have different colored glass to indicate different segments from them on charts.

As they depend on VHF radio signals, VOR beacons have the disadvantage of not being visible over the horizon or behind obstacles such as mountains.

WAAS: Wide Area Augmentation System
See GPS.

Wake Turbulence
Like ships, airliners can produce a troublesome wake, but in their case, it is a swirling coil-like wake coming off the wing tips. Aircraft caught up in it can be jolted and even destabilized, with small aircraft being particularly vulnerable.

It may surprise some to learn that it is more persistent and hence dangerous in calm conditions. In blustery conditions the rotating coils are soon broken up

Again, it is worst when emanating from large airliners climbing in Clean Configuration when laden with fuel just after takeoff. Such was the case in 2001, when an Airbus taking off from New York's JFK airport was caught up in the wake of a Japan Airlines 747 climbing out in clean configuration laden with much fuel for the long flight to Tokyo. The pilot flying the Airbus overreacted and fatally swished off the tail with his extreme too-and-fro rudder inputs.

Air Traffic controllers determine the separation required on landing and takeoff according to the weight of the airliner. It seems the 767 has a notoriously bad wake for its weight, whereas the super-jumbo Airbus 380 is proving better than first feared in this regard.

Washington D.C.
U.S. capital city, not to be confused with Washington <u>State</u> situated in the Pacific Northwest of the country. The letters D.C. stand for District of Columbia, a special Federal district. Boeing had its headquarters in Seattle in Washington State before moving it to Chicago, and still has many of its most important facilities there.

Wicks
Looking like pieces of string, these are attached to the trailing edges of the wings and other airfoils (aerofoils) to dissipate static electricity that might affect the avionics or cause other trouble. They are not designed to handle lightning and are in fact liable to be damaged by it.

Whiteout
A situation found in polar regions where snow on the ground and the absence of shadows and the presence of cloud makes the pilot unable to identify the horizon or a even looming mountain.
A notorious case was the Air New Zealand DC-10 on a sightseeing flight in the Antarctic that had been mistakenly pre-programmed to fly into Mount Erebus in 1979. Whiteout prevented the pilots from seeing it.

Windscreen/Windshield
Windscreens have to be very strong and very high tech.

Even so, windscreens have been known to crack. In one well-publicized case in the U.K., a windscreen panel blew out after maintenance staff used the wrong bolts. The captain was sucked halfway out, and only prevented from disappearing completely by the copilot and subsequently a flight attendant grabbing and holding onto his legs. The aircraft landed successfully with the captain having various injuries including some frostbite, but subsequently being able to return to duty. The flight attendant was not so lucky, with frostbite and eye damage.

Winglet

Mini-wings inclined at various angles attached to the wingtips to improve airflow, give greater lift and fuel efficiency and incidentally but very usefully lessen wake turbulence.

Where handling space at airports may limit wingspan they can be a means whereby carrying capacity/range may be increased.

While not being quite what one might consider winglets to be, the raked wingtips that the A350 and most Boeing 787s will use are wingtip-type devices giving more lift for the same span.

Wiring & Wi-Fi (Special Wave Band)

There are miles of wire on an airliner, posing the problems of weight, possible short-circuits and fire, and complexity.

Just as Wi-Fi reduces the number of wires trailing around ones home or office, tentative plans are afoot to use Wi-Fi for the many non-essential systems on airliners. However, to do this without interference from passengers' electronic equipment, it is necessary to have an internationally allocated exclusive wave band for intra-aircraft use. Unfortunately, getting agreement and international designation of an exclusive wave band takes time. See IFE (In-Flight Entertainment).

Worst-ever Air Accidents

The severity of an accident tends to be judged in terms of the death toll, making it somewhat meaningless as an indication of risks to an individual passenger travelling on that airline or aircraft since the toll is largely determined by the passenger capacity of the aircraft and the load factor(s).

- **The worst-ever air accident involving multiple aircraft in which 583 people died [KLM-Pan Am, Tenerife 1977]**

  The two Boeing 747s collided in fog on the runway.

  A bomb scare at Las Palmas airport in the Canary Islands had resulted in controllers diverting airliners heading there to the relatively small Tenerife Los Rodeos Airport on a neighboring island. When the all clear was given aircraft waiting there began to take off for Las Palmas. With the taxiways blocked by parked aircraft, two 747s (a KLM and a Pan Am) were having to back-taxi in fog up the runway in order to take off. The KLM 747 in the lead got to the end, and after duly making a 180-degree turn, prepared for takeoff, mistakenly believing the PAN Am 747 had already turned off onto a slipway well behind as instructed by the controller.

To cap a series of unfortunate coincidences and missed opportunities to preclude disaster, the Dutch copilot finally said to the controller:

We are at takeoff, which in his mind meant (in Dutch idiom) *We are in the process of* taking off, when in everyone else's mind, it simply meant they were at the takeoff position and about to take off.

The Pan Am pilots, unaware that the KLM aircraft had already started its takeoff run, thought it nevertheless advisable to get out of the way, with the captain saying *Let's get the f..k out of here!* They then through the fog saw the lights of the KLM 747 bearing down on them. They prayed that it would lift off in time, but heavily loaded with newly loaded fuel to ensure a timely return to Amsterdam that evening from Las Palmas, it lifted only enough for the nose to pass over, with the low-slung engines and wheels too low to avoid striking the Pan Am's hump and wing. The KLM 747 continued on, and crashed down on the runway, exploding in a ball of fire with no survivors. A number of those on the Pan Am craft were more fortunate.

- **The worst-ever air accident involving a single aircraft in which 500 people died [Japan Airlines JL123, Japan 1985]**

The rear bulkhead of the almost full Boeing 747 failed with the resultant rush of air blowing off the vertical stabilizer (tail fin) and rudder.

Virtually out of control, with the pilots desperately trying to maneuver using engine power alone, the jumbo staggered around drunkenly for half an hour with passengers writing last wishes on their boarding passes, before crashing into a mountain just after dusk. Because of the difficult terrain, weather and darkness—and perhaps to some extent the expectation that no one could have survived—rescuers only reached the crash site the following morning. In fact, four female passengers survived, including a twelve-year-old girl with merely a sprained wrist. Had help come immediately, a few more passengers in the broken off rear section would have certainly survived—showing that in even the direst of accidents one should expect there to be survivors.

See *Air Crashes and Miracle Landings.*

X-, Y-, Z-axes

Aircraft make angular movements about three axes. They roll or bank about the longitudinal or x-axis (i.e. One wing goes up and the other down.); they pitch about the y-axis running through the wings (i.e. Up and down movement of the nose.); and they yaw about the z-axis (i.e. Turning movement to left or right, sometimes referred to as the *compass direction*).

Yaw

Term used to express an often-involuntary swerve of the aircraft to the left or right. For example, ingestion of birds into an engine on taking off will make the aircraft tend to yaw to that side. Pilots can redress such a yaw by application of the rudder, provided the airspeed of the aircraft is high enough for it to be effective. This is one reason why they do not take off at the first moment they could lift off and allow the airspeed to build up further before doing so.

Zulu (G.M.T./UTC)

In the nineteen-fifties, Z was used to denote Greenwich Mean Time, and as Zulu stands for Z in the NATO Alphabet Letter Enunciation table, it is the word used to denote G.M.T., or rather UTC (Coordinated Universal Time).

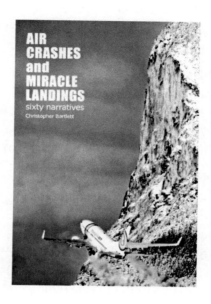

TABLE OF CONTENTS

(Subject to Modification)

Lightning Source UK Ltd.
Milton Keynes UK
28 July 2010
157535UK00002B/16/P